HOW TO
SAIL ON A
BUDGET

ALASTAIR BUCHAN

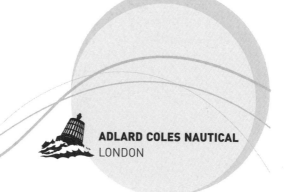

ADLARD COLES NAUTICAL
LONDON

Published by Adlard Coles Nautical
an imprint of A & C Black (Publishers) Ltd
36 Soho Square, London W1D 3QY
www.adlardcoles.com

First published 2009

ISBN 978-0-7136-8889-4

A CIP catalogue record for this book is available from the British Library.

This book is produced using paper that is made from wood grown in
managed, sustainable forests. It is natural, renewable and recyclable.
The logging and manufacturing processes conform to the environmental
regulations of the country of origin.

Typeset in 10.5/12pt ITC Garamond and Scala Sans by
Falcon Oast Graphic Art Ltd

Printed and bound in Great Britain
by Caligraving Ltd, Thetford, Norfolk

Note: while all reasonable care has been taken in the publication of this
edition, the publisher takes no responsibility for the use of the methods
or products described in the book.

Acknowledgements

Every book is a team effort and thanks are due to many people who helped
in the writing of this book. In particular I owe thanks to Bill Ross who
guided me through the detail of painting all types of hulls, and John Noble
whose encyclopaedic knowledge on matters marine has proved invaluable.
Thanks are also due to Janet Murphy at Adlard Coles, to Liz without
whose support it would never happen, and to HLW for reasons she knows
best.

Contents

Introduction

In the current economic climate you may ask yourself: 'Can I afford to go sailing?' It has the reputation for being an expensive sport – but it doesn't have to be. There are many ways that the canny sailor can save money both in his choice of boat and in his sailing style. There are plenty of bargains to be found out there; you just need to do plenty of research and really know what you are looking for. Don't be tempted into an impulse buy. The owner may be offering it at a knock-down price – but there may be a very good reason for this. My chapter on DIY surveying will guide you through the minefield of initial boat selection and will help you to save money straight away by avoiding bad boats.

Reducing the drain on your wallet demands effort. After making the big obvious savings on buying a decent boat in good condition at a reasonable price, and finding an economical mooring, you will then have to work hard to make reasonable savings on maintenance and refits. However, you can possibly recoup some of your expenses by chartering. Some live-aboards pay their way across the oceans by spending part of each year taking paying guests on short cruises. Others use their boats to give sea time and instruction to those wishing to gain experience and sailing qualifications. To do this you must have a suitable yacht and there are countless expensive regulations, insurance costs and other expenses, so you really need to do a business plan to see if it is cost-effective. Also, running a combination of cruise ship and sea school is very hard work!

Alternatively, you could sell your skills aboard someone else's boat, either as professional crew or, if you are experienced and qualified enough, teaching the ropes to new boat owners. If you are confident of your abilities offshore you could undertake yacht deliveries abroad. But again this is hard work and has its own maze of rules and regulations.

The rest of us have to accept that, like any pastime, sailing carries a price tag. This book aims to show you how to keep costs to the minimum. For most of us, cutting down on labour charges represents a huge saving on the annual maintenance bill, but there has to be a balance: if you can earn more per hour self-employed than it costs to fix the boat then pay a professional. It is important to keep a sense of proportion. We sail for pleasure and relaxation. Do not let penny-pinching become an end in itself.

If your aim is to sail on a budget then this book will give you a head start on how to get into the way of economical and cash-sensible thinking that will serve you well for years to come.

What type of sailing will | 1 you do?

My advice is to choose a boat that you can afford and which suits your type of sailing. No boat is suitable for all types of sailing. Being human, at different times we expect to jump aboard our boat and to race, day sail, bluewater cruise, or simply potter. Sometimes we sail alone or with friends or family. Your choice of boat is what you believe is the best compromise between your range of sailing activities. This is a very personal decision.

To make the right choice of boat, it helps to ask the right questions and the following questionnaire tries to list the points you must juggle when making a decision. It is not a formula but a guide that lists the points you ought to consider. There are no scores to add up, no trick questions or right or wrong answers, but when you reach the end you should have built up a profile of your type of sailing and gathered some ideas towards the type of boat you want.

◆ SAILING EXPERIENCE

1	Never sailed before
2	Less than one season
3	Two or three seasons
4	Five to ten years
5	Over ten years

If you have already owned boats or sailed on other people's boats then you will have definite opinions about the boat you want. The longer you have been sailing, the firmer your opinions will be on this matter. If you are new to sailing then your knowledge about boats is likely to be based on adverts, boats reviews and word of mouth. Be aware that no one speaks unkindly of their present boat and that boat reviews often resort to coded language to hint at drawbacks. Adverts by yacht builders and brokers are hardly likely to highlight flaws in the products they promote.

◆ WHAT TYPE OF SAILING

1	Exploring the coastline
2	Racing exclusively
3	Cruising exclusively
4	Cruising with the occasional race
5	Racing with the occasional cruise

Boats perform best at what they are designed to do. You can cruise in a racing yacht or race a cruising yacht but it is hard work. If you enjoy exploring less frequented waters, the absence of shore facilities puts onboard comfort and facilities at a premium. If you gunkhole then you need a boat that can take the ground. Buying the wrong sort of boat for your principal activity is never a wise move, however cheaply the boat is priced.

◆ HOW OFTEN DO YOU EXPECT TO SAIL?

1	Daysail every couple of months
2	Daysail once or twice a month
3	Daysail every weekend
4	Daysail every weekend, sleeping aboard occasionally
5	Sail every weekend and two or three evenings each week
6	Sail every weekend and two or three evenings each week and make one- or two-week cruises each season
7	Extended cruises lasting several weeks or months
8	Live aboard
9	Never sail at night
10	Sail at night once or twice a season
11	Sail at night five to ten times per season
12	Sail at night as required

The more frequently you sail, the closer you should keep your boat to where you live, otherwise too much time, and money, is spent on the road between home and mooring. If you only daysail, then the onboard facilities can be basic. Sleeping on board begins with a cockpit tent or a cabin large enough to contain bunks, a galley of sorts, heads, and electrical power for domestic as well as navigational use. If you make overnight passages, then you should be able to use the galley, heads and bunks at sea. The longer you live aboard, the more space, equipment and home comforts you need. On the other hand, if you buy a boat that is bigger or better equipped than is needed then you are wasting money.

◆ WHERE WILL YOU SAIL?

1	Exclusively on rivers and canals
2	On inland and non-tidal waters
3	Within 5nm of your home port
4	Within two hours of a safe harbour or anchorage
5	Coastal passages of 6–8 hours' duration
6	Coastal passage of over 8 hours' duration
7	Offshore passages
8	Ocean passages
9	Coastal passages in a different area each season

If you sail on inland waters, your boat may have to meet local regulations in terms of fitting out and equipment and be certified to this effect. Check that your boat complies or, if it does not, that the work to bring it up to standard will not break the bank.

On most coastal passages, there are harbours of refuge en route where you can seek shelter in good time if the weather turns unkind, but on offshore passages you may have to take what comes, and your boat should be fitted out to stay at sea in most weathers. If you plan any ocean voyages, your boat must be able to stay at sea in any weather. If you wish to make coastal passages in a different area each season then consider a trailer sailer to cut down on the days, or even weeks, spent reaching your chosen cruising ground.

◆ SAILING IN COMPANY

1	Alone
2	With family
3	With friends

Solo sailing demands easy sail handling and some form of reliable auto-pilot but you have more freedom to decide when and where you sail. If you rely on friends as crew then when you sail depends on everyone co-ordinating their free time. Children aboard limit the type of passage you make and become bored looking at waves. Family sailing is nearly always shorthanded sailing and arrangements aboard should reflect this. The more people who expect to sleep on board regularly the bigger the boat you will need.

◆ YOUR HOME PORT

1	Within two hours' travel from your home
2	Two to four hours' travel
3	Over four hours' travel

The further you live from your boat the less likely you are to sail for an evening or on impulse and the more money you spend travelling between home and boat.

◆ ACCESS TO YOUR HOME PORT

1	Available at all states of tide and in any weather
2	Available for at least half the tide and most weathers
3	Available for an hour or less either side of high water
4	Harbour car parking is secure and convenient
5	Harbour car parking is difficult and/or expensive

If access to your home port is limited by tides or bridge or lock-opening times, you can rule out regular evening or weekend sailing. It is worth checking out the parking facilities shoreside. Returning on the midnight tide you do not want to be faced with a locked car park, a three-mile trudge to your car or, worst of all, no car.

◆ TYPE OF BERTH

1	Pontoon
2	A swinging mooring
3	A fore-and-aft mooring or trot
4	Your back garden

A pontoon berth cannot be beaten for convenience. A swinging or trot mooring can add up to an hour, sometimes more, for ferrying crew and kit to and from the boat at the start and end of each passage. Even allowing for launching fees, parking your boat at home for all or much of the year is a good reason to consider a trailer sailer.

◆ PORT FACILITIES

1	Good facilities for lifting your boat out of the water
2	Good facilities for launching and recovering trailer sailers
3	Lift-out and launching facilities are available only by special arrangement
4	Good facilities for working on your boat during refit
5	Limited facilities for working on your boat during refit
6	No facilities for working on your boat

Limited facilities at your home port may mean having to take your boat somewhere else for winter storage. If lift-out is by special arrangement, it may be expensive and if there is no power available then working on the boat during the winter could be difficult and expensive. Some marinas insist that maintenance work is carried out by their approved contractors which keeps your costs and their profits high.

◆ PRACTICAL SKILLS

1	You have good woodworking skills
2	You are competent at working in GRP
3	You can weld steel, including stainless steel
4	You can weld aluminium

5	You can maintain marine engines
6	You can fit electrical equipment
7	You can fit and maintain LPG appliances
8	You can splice rope and wire
9	You have a good working knowledge of paints and coatings

Maintenance is labour intensive and the more you do then the more money you save. Buy a boat whose construction and equipment matches your practical skills.

◆ RUNNING COSTS

Make a realistic estimate of how much you can afford for your boat's annual running costs. Do not try to offset any part of these against the price of your annual holiday and, unless you plan to live aboard, changing your lifestyle to save money is an illusion. If you are planning to sail on a shoestring then you must carefully research the running costs of the boat you intend to buy.

Only you know what compromises you can accept and still balance the conflicting demands of:

- How much you can afford to spend on a boat
- How much you can afford to spend on its upkeep
- What you want the boat to do
- Where you want to sail
- The time you have available to sail

Inconsistencies in your answers point towards areas where you may have to downsize your ambitions. Ignore discrepancies at your peril. They turn dreams into nightmares.

The search for a suitable boat begins by deciding whether you wish to:

- Sail other people's boats
- Buy a new boat
- Buy a second-hand boat
- Build one yourself
- Refit a yacht in need of major repair
- Make your boat pay its way

◆ SAILING OTHER PEOPLE'S BOATS

You do not need to own a boat in order to go sailing. The costs of buying, berthing and maintaining a boat can be avoided by sailing other people's boats. You may never be skipper but a good crew member is a pearl beyond price and can pick and choose when and where they sail. Some keen skippers will even bribe experienced crew by paying all their expenses.

Boats looking for crew or crew looking for boats find each other through friends, club notice boards and crewing agencies.

◆ CHARTER

If you wish to skipper a yacht without the expense of owning your own boat and are prepared to limit your sailing to two or three weeks a year, then chartering works out much cheaper than boat ownership. In addition to freeing you from berthing fees and annual maintenance costs, chartering also opens up the possibility of exploring overseas cruising grounds. Some sailing clubs own yachts that their members can charter cheaply. If that is not available to you there is always commercial charter.

◆ TYPES OF CHARTER

Bareboat charter

A bareboat charter is not a boat stripped to basics but chartering a boat and sailing without a company skipper on board. Before letting you loose, the charter company will need to be reassured that you can handle the boat safely. Normally the minimum seagoing qualification for bareboat charter is a full (Shorebased Theory and Practical) RYA Yachtmaster™ Coastal certificate or an acceptable equivalent.

Skippered charter

If you, or the company, have doubts about your ability then you may wish, or the company may insist, that you hire a professional skipper for the trip. There will then be an additional charge of about two-thirds of the charter cost.

Flotilla sailing

A flotilla cruise is a halfway house between a bareboat and skippered charter. You skipper but sail in convoy with a number of other boats, one of which is skippered by the convoy leader who is on hand to offer advice and help. Charges for flotilla sailing are normally per person and include travel costs.

Boatshare

This is a variation on mantime timeshare for those who feel competent to bareboat charter. For a fixed monthly fee you are promised a certain number of weeks a year sailing. There may be an annual membership fee and a requirement to give several months' notice if you wish to quit. The weekly rate is around 40 per cent of a fortnight's bareboat charter which makes it attractive but as most people wish to take an annual cruise in July and August there may be restrictions on availability and the commitment to a monthly fee makes shopping around an expensive option if you cannot get your preferred dates. If you can only manage a couple of weeks sailing a year then a boatshare scheme becomes an expensive option.

The cost of charter

It is difficult to compare costs. On paper, boatshare schemes offer the cheapest weekly sailing but making this a reality may require sailing at inconvenient and unpopular times of year. Flotilla sailing for a family of four may appear much more expensive than bareboat but the cost per person usually includes flights and when these are added to bareboat costs the figures become closer.

Finally, prices may be quoted in currencies other than sterling and currency fluctuations can see prices swing up and down without warning. The figures in the table on page 9 give comparative costs for different types of charter. The prices are those for high season which coincides with the school holidays. As always, term-time holidays are cheaper. On flotilla holidays there may be a discount of around 10 per cent for anyone under 16. Some companies offer discounts for repeat bookings and there may also be a discount if you book within a week of the start of your cruise.

Some companies offer a midweek charter option which may be attractive if you are planning a one-week cruise. Instead of Friday to Friday as in a weekly charter, a midweek charter is usually Sunday evening to Friday evening. It adds up to five days' sailing instead of seven but if you live several hours' travel from where the boat is lying and cannot leave work on Friday in time to take over the boat on Friday, then it may be Saturday afternoon before you are ready to sail.

Normally when winds of force 6 or more are blowing or forecast the charter is postponed or if the charter has begun then you stay in harbour. Prolonged poor weather at the start of a cruise may result in cancellation. Depending on the company there may be a full or partial refund or the offer of alternative dates. When going abroad, check on the weather patterns you can expect. Some companies in the Caribbean have their high season charges during the hurricane season when the risk of losing a cruise to poor weather is high.

COMPARING TYPICAL CHARTER COSTS

LOA	Bareboat two-week cruise	Flotilla two-week cruise	Boatshare 7 weeks' sailing
32ft (9.7m)	£2,904	£4,486	£4,987
35ft (10.6m)	£4,085	£4,988	£6,187
39ft (11.8m)	£5,379	£5,272	£7,387

Extra costs

Check what is included in the price. Some charter companies include a tank of fuel and a bottle of gas, others do not. A deposit, usually into four figures, against late return, damage or loss is required before you set sail. Some charterers insist you also take out an additional hull damage waiver insurance and the cost of this premium is not returnable. They may require the dinghy and outboard to be insured separately.

Travel costs

Bareboat charters do not normally include travel between home and the boat but flotilla cruises, which tend to take place in sunny climes, normally include travel between a designated airport and the boat. Travel between home and the airport, accommodation en route and transfer between airport and boat abroad are usually extras.

◆ BUYING NEW

Buying new is attractive. For a little extra cash you have a fault-free boat fitted out to your specification with the promise of several years' low maintenance. If it holds its value, the extra outlay of buying new may be recouped when you come to sell.

Nowadays 'new' nearly always means buying a boat built on a production line and marketed through a network of distributors rather than directly from a yard. Your own specification means mixing and matching from a list of manufacturer's options on rig, keel, deck, engine and internal layout. Choosing anything but the basic, standard production boat pushes the price up.

The next shock to your wallet is that you are expected to pay for its delivery to the distributor. Then comes a commissioning charge for unpacking the boat, stepping the mast, firing up the engine and applying a coat of antifouling. Most costly of all, new boats, even sail-away versions, lack the basic equipment that allows you to sail away in a safe and seamanlike manner. By the time you have paid the extra charges, bought and fitted the absolute minimum of gear and added taxes, the price gap between new and second-hand resembles a financial Grand Canyon and you are unlikely to totally recover the extra outlay that buying new demands when you come to sell. So a new boat is not really a viable option for the budget sailor.

◆ BUYING SECOND-HAND

Buying a second hand boat is the cheapest way of getting afloat in your own boat, particularly if you are new to sailing. The inevitable bumps, bangs and scrapes of a steep learning curve add only to those the boat already has and are not quite as painful to your bank balance as repairing a new boat.

On the downside, every second-hand boat has a history. You do not know how it has been sailed and maintained; what modifications have been made, or if it has been damaged or even sunk. At the end of each hurricane season in the Caribbean, a lot of boats which have spent time on the bottom of a hurricane hole, suddenly, and in suspiciously good condition, appear on the market.

On the plus side, most second-hand boats come with an inventory of kit that lets you start sailing right away. Even so, it is prudent to earmark at least 10–15 per cent of your budget to replace ageing equipment, worn sails and tired rigging. During the next two or three seasons, set aside a percentage of your annual budget for a phased upgrading programme.

It is possible to get afloat in a boat that will take you across oceans for little more than the cost of buying and owning a second-hand car. But where do you direct your cost-cutting efforts so that you make the greatest return for the least effort? Spending pounds to save pennies is not good sense. Savings on refit, mooring and cruising roll in year after year while those on buying the boat and personal gear are one offs, but if they are amortised over five years then more than 90 per cent of your expenditure is on buying a boat and mooring fees.

WHERE THE MONEY GOES

	New boat budget (%)	Second-hand boat budget (%)
Cost of boat	69	84
Delivery to agent	1	1
Delivery to home port	3	1
Commissioning	3	3
Insurance	3	2
Equipment	6	10
Taxes	15	

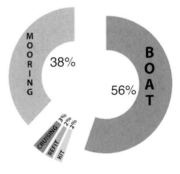

◆ BUILD YOUR OWN BOAT

Building your own boat is a good way of owning the biggest boat possible for the least amount of cash. Many sailors have successfully chosen this route and produced professional-quality boats. But before you take this route, do your research very carefully because building your own boat is a major project and not as straightforward as it first appears. There are no figures available but anecdotal evidence suggests that for every DIY boat started, at least three or four are never finished. Also, cost and build time often rise unexpectedly. A rough rule of thumb is: before starting work, double your estimated costs and multiply the projected build time by four.

The site where you build your dream boat is one of the hidden costs of self-building. Ideally this should be under cover with easy access to power and water and space to securely store materials and equipment. You want a location as near your home as possible so that you can work in the evenings and at weekends without hours of travelling. If you do not have a yard of your own then you will have to rent suitable space. If this is a corner of a boatyard instead of inside a shed, then cover from the elements will probably be a scaffolding tent and secure storage space will be an old shipping container. One way or another, you will be paying out rather more money than you first expected for several years.

DIY has the advantage of paying-as-you-build which allows you to pause or accelerate the building programme to suit your cash flow. You must factor into your budget that a home-built boat has a lower second-hand value than an equivalent professionally-built boat even if the home-built boat is constructed and fitted out to a higher standard.

DIY GUIDELINES
Preparations and planning   Before starting work, seek advice from those who have already successfully built a boat, and in your planning make generous allowances for unexpected delays and unforeseen costs.
Skills required   Boat building requires a wide range of skills, not just in whatever material you choose for the hull and deck. These include carpentry, engineering, plumbing, heating, electrical and electronics. If you do not have these skills, learn them or acquire a wide circle of skilled friends who are prepared to work for coffee and cakes.
Budget   Prepare and price all the materials and equipment you need; find suppliers and include their delivery charges in your costs. At this stage, multiply estimated costs by three.

Scale of savings   Savings on raw materials and items such as masts, rigging, sails, blocks and winches are low to non-existent. Most savings come from your free labour. If you paid yourself the minimum wage the final price would scare your bank manager and bankrupt you. Savings in the form of paying less than you would for a similar professionally-built boat do not turn into profit. The second-hand value of a home-built boat is usually lower than that of the equivalent production boat.

Insurance   As your investment grows, insurance becomes essential. Insurance on home-built boats is normally higher than for production yachts.

Tools and equipment   A good range of professional quality hand and power tools is required. These are not cheap.

Yard space   You need a yard or at least a space where you can work and store materials, tools and equipment securely. Under solid cover is much better than building a scaffolding tent. If you are renting building space, include this cost in your budget. If you have no secure store you will need a van to carry materials and equipment back and forth.

Utilities   You need reliable access to water and electrical power either from the mains supply or from a generator. During winter months you need industrial-quality heating.

Timescale   Unless you are boatbuilding full time, most self-build projects take several years to complete. Your initial timescale is always optimistic; multiply it by four.

DIY kit boats

DIY kit boats are professionally part-built. Options range from buying an empty hull to having the manufacturer fit the bulkheads and join the hull and deck together. Some manufacturers even supply the hulls, decks and bulkheads finished and all the other bits and pieces ready cut and shaped to complete the boat. Kit boats are more expensive than self-build but you get afloat much quicker and it is still cheaper than buying a new finished boat, although probably more expensive than the equivalent second-hand boat.

◆ REFITTING A YACHT IN NEED OF MAJOR REPAIR

This option is generally taken by those who have found the classic boat of their dreams which has been allowed to fall into disrepair; they are prepared to lavish almost unlimited time and cash restoring the yacht to

FITTING OUT A GRP HULL A common mistake when buying a hull to fit out is to choose the biggest your money will buy. You will then learn the hard way how much cash, time and effort is needed to add a deck and make the hull habitable. Carefully price the entire project *before* you purchase the hull. Do not forget that when it is finished, its running costs are the same as for any other boat of its size.

pristine condition. The finished product will be worth much more than it cost to buy but not as much as has been paid out to rebuild it.

However, it is possible that you may find a boat which is in poor condition but is essentially sound and can be made seaworthy with some effort and little expenditure. It is much more likely that you will come across a part completed home-built or kit boat whose present owner has run out of cash or enthusiasm, or both, and wishes to cut his losses. These failed projects are often available for a fraction of the cash you would need to pay out to reach the same stage of construction and frequently come with many of the bits and pieces needed for their completion. Provided the work done so far is to a satisfactory standard, and you have the skills to complete the job, then they represent a cheap way for the budget sailor to get afloat.

◆ COMPARING PRICES

It is fairly straightforward to work out where the cash goes when buying a new or second-hand boat. The figures show that when you buy second-hand you can afford to spend around 30 per cent more of your budget on the boat. This is because you need to buy less equipment and there are savings on taxes. (See tables below.)

DISTRIBUTION OF EXPENDITURE WHEN BUYING A SECOND-HAND BOAT

Item	Percentage of budget
Cost of boat	83.6
Haul-out and survey	0.8
Settlement and documentation	0.5
Delivery	1.5
Insurance of the vessel	1.3
Refit and equipment	10.0
Taxes	2.5
TOTAL	100.0

DISTRIBUTION OF EXPENDITURE WHEN BUYING A NEW BOAT

Item	Percentage of budget
Boat	62.5
Delivery to agent	0.6
Delivery to home port	1.5
Commissioning	1.3
Insurance	1.6
Equipment	15.0
Taxes	17.5
TOTAL	100.0

STEEL DIY HULL The original boatbuilder built the hull, painted it, put in the bulk-heads, fitted the deck and then stopped work. After several years he sold it for a song complete with mast, boom, standing rigging and brand-new engine. If you have the practical skills, a boat like this is one of the cheapest means of getting afloat but finding this sort of project takes patience mixed with luck.

Looking at the cost of DIY boats, kit boats and major refitting projects, the picture is less clear. This is mostly because some expenditure never appears on the books. It would be unusual to include an hourly figure for your own labour in the expenditure, or the cost of travelling between the boat and home, or the extra meals you eat out, or the occasional item you buy on the way to the boat. If they were added in, then the final bill would be frighteningly high. However, anecdotal evidence suggests that by counting only the cash paid out, self-build probably just wins the race to be the cheapest way of getting afloat.

It is only just ahead of buying a second-hand boat where you have the advantages of purchasing a known product, avoiding much hard labour and getting afloat several years earlier.

◆ CAN YOUR BOAT EARN ITS KEEP?

Boats can be made to pay their way but before you take this route there are some important points to consider:

1   Check if the authorities will regard your boat as a commercial craft. If so, discover what additional work is necessary to bring it up to

commercial standards and if it needs to be officially certified. It is also possible that you may require the appropriate professional qualifications to act as skipper with paying customers aboard.

2 Inform your insurance company. Most insurance policies contain a clause excluding using your boat as a business. Similarly, your berthing agreement may exclude commercial activities.

3 If opting for bareboat charter, think about how you ensure that your customers are competent. This is not just to make sure they do not damage your boat. You have a legal duty of care to check that their nautical ambitions are in step with their abilities.

4 Do you have the time to manage the administration that a working boat brings, such as the advertising, booking and the meeting and greeting of clients?

Putting your boat out to charter

If you own a boat then putting it out to charter is one way of reducing costs. Chartering comes in different forms, ranging from bareboat charters to corporate entertainment.

If you choose bareboat charter then there are companies which, for a fee, do all administration, including the handover and handing back of the boat and some even offer to look after berthing and annual maintenance.

Timeshare

Some charter companies offer yachting timeshare holidays. You buy a yacht of a type and specification that they lay down. They will then include the boat in their charter fleet and, in return, you are given an agreed number of days sailing on your own or a similar boat plus a guaranteed income.

Cost sharing

Asking your crew to contribute towards their time aboard probably escapes being classed as a commercial activity either by the authorities or your insurance company and it does, at least, reduce your cruising costs.

3 | Choosing the right boat

It does not always follow that once you know what kind of sailing yo
want to do then the type of boat you need is self-evident. Whether you rad
or cruise there are still choices to make.

◆ RACING YACHTS

Every step of a racing yacht's design, construction and fitting out aims t
make it go as fast and as close to the wind as possible. Hull, spars an
rigging are made of lightweight expensive materials, and a different high
tech sail is needed for every change in wind strength or direction. Racin
yachts are driven hard. Equipment has a brutal, short working life. A fres
design concept, or the introduction of new materials or gadgets, results i
a costly refit.

Racing means joining a club and buying a class boat that fits their rad

Club racers are characterised by
narrow coachroofs, wide side decks,
hank-on or foil foresails and open-
stern cockpits to aid self-draining.
These are exciting but demanding
boats to sail but keeping them
competitive is not cheap.

programme. This narrows choice and determines your budget. If you buy a type of boat not raced by your club you may still be able to race on handicap and can travel around the country to rallies of boats of the same class.

By definition, second-hand racing yachts are last year's models and no longer lead the fleet. Although they can be bought quite cheaply, the need for regular upgrades to keep them competitive keeps their running costs as high, or higher, than those of a new racer. What scope there is for savings comes from picking the right mooring, doing as much of the annual refit yourself and buying the right personal equipment.

Racing yachts can be divided into dinghies, keel boats and club racers.

Racing dinghies

Modern racing dinghies need fair levels of competence and physical fitness to sail them competitively. They are a young person's boat and, although they are the least expensive form of racing, they are not cheap. A state-of-the-art machine with a decent set of sails, road trailer and launching trolley costs as much as a small to medium-sized cruising yacht. With few exceptions, building your own to save money is not an option. It is important to check that boats fully comply with class rules. Unauthorised modifications will be picked up by race scrutinisers and are expensive to correct. Between races, dinghies live in the club dinghy park or at the back of the garage, both of which keeps berthing costs low.

When not racing, keel boats spend most of their days on their trailer. Lacking self-draining cockpits they need a cockpit tent if they are not to fill up with rainwater. This is a Squib.

Racing keel boats

Keel boats are large dinghies with a fixed, ballasted keel such as Flying Fifteens, Dragons, Solings and Tempests or local classes like the Loch Long on the Clyde in Scotland. They demand less gymnastic ability to sail than dinghies, which explains their appeal to the more mature, deep-pocketed sailor. None are cheap. Between races, keel boats lie to a pontoon, on a mooring or are lifted out onto a trailer.

KEELS
It is possible for otherwise identical hulls to have completely different keel configurations. It is beyond the scope of this book to discuss the merits of different keel types but if you keep your boat on a drying mooring or 'ditch crawl' with the ever-present possibility of involuntarily taking the ground, then you want a keel that lets a boat sit on the mud without falling over. In practice this means either a bilge or lifting keel.
On some GRP boats, bilge keels may be glassed into the hull. If so, the bottom of the keel should be protected against grounding. The upwind performance of bilge keels is, supposedly, below that of fin or lifting keels, but on small boats this is academic.
Lifting keels may pivot or be a dagger board travelling vertically. Its weight may contribute to the ballast. Some lifting keels even have a heavy bulb or wings at their foot. In the cabin the box which houses the keel is usually disguised as a table. On larger boats raising and lowering the keel is done by electric motors which adds to the complexity and cost.
On trailer sailers, water ballast is normally used which is dumped as the boat comes out of the water. This keeps the towing weight as low as possible. Lifting keels on these boats do not normally form part of the ballast.

Club racer

The average club racer is 22–35ft (6.7–10.6m) LOA and is sailed like a dinghy. The only reason the crew sit out on the rail and are not hanging on trapezes during races is that the rules prohibit it. To save weight, the fitting out below decks is the minimum required under class rules. To the untrained eye this looks like a bare hull, fit for nothing but sail stowage. Lack of facilities is not a problem as most races last no more than a day, often less, and the crew expect to spend their time on deck.

◆ CRUISING YACHTS

Cruising yachts spend more time at sea and make longer passages than racing yachts but they are rarely driven hard. This means that they age better. For this reason, an old cruising boat is a better buy than an old racing yacht. Simplistic descriptions like entry-level boat, day boat, weekender, estuary cruiser, pocket cruiser, holiday cruiser, offshore cruiser, voyager and bluewater cruiser tramlines your thinking and closes down options. One person's weekender is another's bluewater cruiser. In the UK, small and medium-sized cruisers make up 75 per cent of the market and this is where you will have the greatest choice of boat.

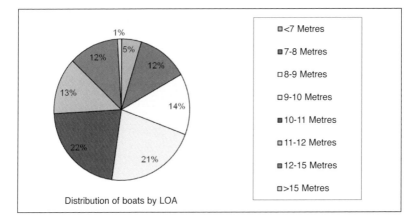

Distribution of boats by LOA

- □ <7 Metres
- ■ 7-8 Metres
- □ 8-9 Metres
- □ 9-10 Metres
- ■ 10-11 Metres
- □ 11-12 Metres
- ■ 12-15 Metres
- □ >15 Metres

The rule of thumb is the larger the boat, the more it costs to buy and to keep. Save money by not buying a boat which is bigger than you need, has facilities you will not use or capabilities beyond your abilities.

Small cruisers

The smallest, and therefore cheapest, cruisers are open boats 15–18ft (4.6–5.5m) LOA. They make great family day boats. Occasionally they are faithful (and expensive) replicas of traditional designs but more often fibreglass imitates their original construction.

Life aboard is primitive. Shelter underway is provided by warm clothing and good waterproofs. A drysuit may prove a better investment than separate oilskin jacket and trousers. Once you become cold or wet, the lack of shelter on open boats brings a very real threat of hypothermia.

Realistically, the range of an open boat is within three or four hours of

Little more than a keel boat with a lid, small cruisers can be great fun. If cash is really short this is one of the best ways of getting afloat as they are cheap to buy, berth and maintain; accommodation is basic.

a harbour. Short daytime coastal passages and a boom tent in harbour each night make longer cruises possible.

The next size up are small cruisers with a cabin 18–24ft (5.5–7.3m) LOA. They have between two and four berths although, in reality, berths can only be used in harbour and then only if everyone goes to bed at the same time. Parents with young children may wish to invest in a decent cockpit tent so in the evening when the children are in bed they can socialise in the cockpit.

Under 21ft (6.4m) LOA, engines are often an outboard of 4–10hp hanging off the stern or in a well. These are less efficient than an inboard engine but cheaper and easier to replace when they reach the end of their working life. Over 21ft (6.4m) LOA, it is normal to fit a small inboard diesel or saildrive engine. Both are more expensive than an outboard engine and should have a second battery dedicated to engine starting.

In settled conditions, small cruisers can easily stay at sea for 12 hours and are well suited to making 20–30-mile coastal passages. Occasional overnight passages should not offer any problems in settled weather.

Medium-sized cruisers

At 24–32ft (7.3–9.7m) LOA there is now enough space for the forepeak to be separated from the main cabin by a couple of bulkheads with the space between them providing a home for a toilet to port and a wet locker to starboard. Standing headroom becomes possible. In harbour, the forepeak

It claims to sleep four, sometimes five, but in reality this medium-sized cruiser provides a comfortable cruising home for two. These boats can be lively in a seaway but even in short lumpy seas they are docile if the sails are properly balanced.

gives the illusion of a double bed while the settees in the main cabin double as bunks. With the addition of good leecloths, these make excellent sea berths. On some boats, quarter berths may take over the cockpit lockers to create a small, separate cabin under the cockpit or something larger in centre cockpit boats.

Coastal and offshore passages should not be a problem, although in heavy weather, upwind progress becomes minimal around force 5, and without the aid of the engine is non-existent somewhere towards the top end of a force 6.

Large cruisers

In strong winds, cruisers in excess of 32–40ft (9.7–12m) LOA have the weight and power to punch through heavy seas and continue on their way rather than travelling sideways like their smaller cousins.

They also have much more living space. Above 40ft (12m) LOA, the curse of having every inch of space serving at least two, perhaps three, incompatible purposes is lifted. Separate ensuite cabins guarantee the privacy essential to civilised life on long cruises.

Larger cruisers tend to have fridges, freezers, watermakers, water heaters, air conditioning, central heating, microwave cookers, washing machines and dishwashers. Life aboard approaches shoreside levels of comfort but at a price, for the equipment that makes it possible is

This cutter-rigged steel-hulled cruiser is a strong, no-nonsense, go any-where boat. The pilot house offers both shelter and good all-round visibility and there is enough room below decks for everyone to have their own living space. It is slow in light winds but comes into its own in heavy weather.

expensive to buy, costly to maintain and so greedy for power that the engine alternator must be supplemented with some combination of generator, wind or solar power.

Large cruisers are easily capable of a warm weather circumnavigation, and a few are able to make the traditional 'three capes' route through the Southern Ocean.

◆ HYBRIDS

In an attempt to be all things to all yachtsmen, some yachts claim to be multi-purpose. The truth of these claims is a matter of judgment. Your opinion is as good as any other.

Cruiser/racer

Depending on your preference, a cruiser/racer may be a racing hull fitted out for cruising or a cruising hull stripped for speed. Neither is as fast as a racing machine or as comfortable as a cruiser but is likely to be competitive on handicap with similar boats. This would be your answer to joining in mid-week and weekend races while still making a summer cruise in relative comfort.

Motor sailer

In return for modest upwind performance, a beamy, boxy hull, reminiscent of a traditional fishing boat, offers more decent living space than a similar-sized yacht. Motor sailers start around 23ft (7m) LOA but most are 30ft (9m) LOA or more. Foot for foot they are more expensive to buy and maintain than a similar sized yacht.

Trailer sailer

Dinghies and most open boats are transported on trailers and the term trailer sailer usually refers to small cruisers, 18-22ft (2.4–6.7m) LOA, with a cabin. Their design is heavily influenced by traffic regulations which dictates the maximum towing dimensions and all-up towed weight which should not exceed 85 per cent of the car's weight. All-up towed weight means not just the weight of the boat but all the gear you have stowed aboard including the engine, fuel, water and other supplies. This can add up to 50 per cent or more of the boat's weight. If you opt for one of the larger trailer sailers then you may need to buy a bigger, more powerful car.

Much over 22ft (6.7m) LOA, any boat becomes too beamy for road transport by trailer and fin and bilge keeled boats sit so high on trailers that they can be difficult to tow, launch and recover. Consequently, the majority of trailer sailing yachts have lifting keels with the centreboard casing taking up valuable living space in the cabin.

If you are looking for small cruiser then these have some very attractive advantages. Escaping marina fees heads the list. Between cruises you can keep your boat on the driveway at home. If there are problems over keeping your boat at home then there are alternatives which will not break the bank. (See Chapter 11)

You will have to pay a fee to launch your boat each time you sail. But if you use your yacht club slip then launching may be free, or an add-on to your membership. Some slipways charge per launch, others offer monthly or seasonal deals; there may be discounts for yacht club members. Even if you

Most trailer sailers are characterised by lightness of construction and a penchant for lifting keels to make launching and recovery as simple as possible. Saving weight can reach extremes. Some reduce their towing weight by taking on water ballast and there is, for example, no bow roller on this model which could make anchoring in heavy weather a problem. Substantial road trailers may overtax the average family car.

sailed every weekend during the season and took holidays afloat, the bill for launching your boat will still be far below the cost of keeping it in a marina.

You will not incur much extra cost in transporting the boat (perhaps a slightly higher fuel bill) as you would probably have to drive to the marina anyway, plus having the boat at home makes working on it between trips or for the winter refit much easier.

Owning a trailer sailer opens up distant cruising grounds. For anyone based on the English south coast, cruising the Western Isles of Scotland involves a week or so of hard sailing before you can start exploring the islands plus the extra cost of overnight fees. With a trailer sailer you can be up in the Highlands and ready to sail within a couple of days.

How far afield you chose to travel is limited by your imagination. One trailer sailer based in the middle of Germany, which is about as far from open water as you can be in Europe, has cruised the Aegean Islands, the Black Sea, the Adriatic, the Baltic and visited the Lofoten Islands.

Since a trailer sailer's mast is designed to be easily stepped and rigged, the low bridges of inland waters hold no fears. Trailer sailers really are a good budget option for all waters.

As a rule, the bigger the multihull, the more living space but this may not hold true for home-builds which may have accommodation in 'his 'n hers' hulls. Professionally-built multihulls are more expensive than comparable-sized monohulls.

◆ MULTIHULLS

You either love or hate multihulls. Supporters claim they are faster, more comfortable and spacious than monohulls and because they lack ballast, they may capsize but never sink. While racing, multihulls are extremely quick but their performance over long passages is similar to that of the same-sized monohull.

What size of boat do | 4 you need?

If your wallet runs to it, then the old saying, 'a foot of boat for every year of your age' remains true for anyone over the age of 20. Sadly, regardless of age, if you are shoestring sailing then large is pricey to buy and run.

As boats grow longer they become fatter. A 40ft (12m) boat is around three times beamier than a 20ft (6m) boat; its working sail area is about four times greater, and its mast over twice as high. Above deck everything is three to four times bigger, heavier and more expensive and below deck there is at least four times the space to be fitted out. On the other hand, a second-hand 20ft (6m) yacht costs about the same as a new winch on a 40ft (12m) boat and its annual running costs, even on the most generous calculation, are less than a quarter.

The easiest way to save money is to buy the smallest boat that meets your requirements. Unfortunately, 'small' is an elusive word to define. It varies with the sailing you do, who you do it with and where it all takes place. Time spent deciding what small means for you before you begin looking for a boat increases the chance of finding the right boat.

◆ SLEEPING ARRANGEMENTS

A large part of defining 'small' depends on the sleeping arrangements. If you are marina-hopping then on passage some bunks can be used as seats or for seabag storage and only become beds in harbour. With a V-berth in the forepeak, a couple of sea berths and minimal onboard facilities, a crew of four aboard a 20–25ft (6–7.6m) yacht can happily spend a couple of weeks cruising from harbour to harbour where regular and easy access to good-quality shore facilities makes modest discomfort all part of the fun.

The same four crew making extended passages need a bigger yacht with better facilities. Once you spend more than 24 hours at sea everyone needs a proper berth of their own and somewhere other than a seabag to stow their kit. The galley must turn out proper meals, not just hot drinks and snacks, and those off watch should be able to rest without being disturbed by those on watch, or at least be able to pull a curtain across their bunk to give an illusion of privacy. There must be a decent toilet, a large

Comfort is not always proportional to size. Looking forward on a 55ft LOA yacht which advertises seven berths, five in the main cabin and two in the forepeak. Tilt this picture 30°, shake it up and down, add seven people plus their kit, and imagine life afloat.

wet locker and stowage for the additional supplies, fuel and water. Your ideal boat has now grown to 35–40ft (10.6–12m) overall with a much higher specification and a matching price increase.

If you are sailing with young children, open plan accommodation can be a disaster. In the evening parents are exiled to the cockpit while the children are in their bunks below. Sleep is the last thing on children's minds. They spend the evening waiting to ambush any adult who looks below to check if they are asleep. A cockpit tent is essential for any sort of social life. Better still, having an aft cabin as a bedroom/playroom gives the children their own space and leaves the rest of the boat free for parents to socialise and sleep, but this means looking at yachts in the over 30ft (9m) range.

◆ COMFORT AND SIZE

Comfort ought to be in direct proportion to size but this is not always the case. Some larger, older boats which look as though they should be able to accommodate their crew in absolute luxury are spartan below decks and life aboard is horribly uncomfortable. A few days' fair weather passage-making leaves their crews looking like shell-shocked battlefield survivors. Bear this in mind when looking at older boats.

Do not confuse size with seaworthiness. The trend is for bluewater boats to be 40ft (12m) LOA or larger but this requirement is not written in stone and often the extra comfort that larger size should bring is lost because of the numbers on board. *Gipsy Moth IV* may not have been particularly cosy when Sir Francis Chichester sailed it round the world but it would be ferociously uncomfortable with five people living aboard.

If you wish to venture onto the oceans and cannot afford a large yacht then the list of small boats that have successfully made bluewater passages is long, and is still growing. Regardless of size, a well-equipped, well-maintained yacht is always more seaworthy than a larger, ill-equipped, poorly-maintained boat. This is because the quality of fitting out of any yacht is directly proportional to the time and cash spent on carrying out the work. It is quicker and cheaper to properly fit out a 20ft (6m) LOA yacht than one that is twice as big; the result is likely to be a boat that is not only more fit for purpose but more comfortable to sail.

5 | What hull material?

Each building material has its proponents who swear by it and each has its disadvantages that they ignore. Ultimately your choice is a very personal decision and reflects not just cost but the sort of boat that you feel happy to sail and maintain.

◆ WOOD

As the number of yards building wooden boats began their near-terminal decline in the 1960s, many classic wooden designs enjoyed a renaissance in GRP. Nowadays, a second-hand wooden boat is either very old and has had

Wooden hulls began going out of favour in the 1960s and 1970s and are now a minority taste. Their lines reflect those of great, classic yachts promising speed (though not by today's standards) and seaworthiness. They are always less roomy below decks than you might first imagine. They can be bought quite cheaply but keeping them seaworthy can be tricky. Out of the water they should be kept under cover. This hull has caught the sun and needs re-caulking before being repainted.

a costly renovation with a price tag to match or requires a huge amount of expensive, skilled restoration. If you want a new wooden hull, it will be a pricey one-off from one of the few remaining yards working in wood.

Plywood is still popular for the hulls of some dinghies and home-built multihulls and there are a few plywood small cruisers such as the Mirror Offshore available.

Maintaining a wooden boat in good condition demands much cash and lots of time. Unless you have the necessary skills this type of boat is not a good option for the budget sailor as the expertise for this work is in short supply and is reflected in very high labour charges. Traditionally, wooden hulls were painted with yacht enamel paints. Nowadays, the hull should be protected by epoxy paints beginning with a primer and working up through an undercoat to several layers of topcoat. Any damage to this coating must be made good as soon as possible to prevent water seeping between the paint and the wood. Owning a wooden boat is more of a love affair than a cheap means of getting afloat.

◆ STEEL

Steel is able to withstand bumps and bangs well but steel boats are heavy, and slow in light winds. As a hull material, steel is generally found only on yachts over 30ft (9m) LOA and almost never on sailing multihulls. Size alone makes professionally-built steel yachts expensive but steel is popular with DIY builders who reckon it gives a large, cheap hull. It is important

Small steel boats exist but usually they start around 30ft (9m) LOA. DIY builders find steel an attractive, strong material that can produce a finished hull in a matter of months but fitting out may take years. Steel hulls are normally boxy but some professional hulls incorporate elegant, sweeping curves.

to protect the hull and deck from rust. A good, multi-layer epoxy paint job probably lasts for five to ten years but this is costly and time-consuming to apply. Good insulation is necessary to prevent condensation inside the hull.

◆ ALUMINIUM

Although aluminium offers the strength of steel with less weight there are comparatively few aluminium boats. Perhaps this is because, unlike steel, it is not a cheap and easily-welded material. There are few DIY aluminium yachts and even when professionally and expensively built, there can be problems with galvanic reaction between different metals. This is most common around deck and hull fittings. Properly built and maintained, there should be no problems but if you wish to buy a second-hand aluminium boat, check it out very carefully.

◆ GRP

Glass reinforced plastic or fibre reinforced plastic is also known as fibreglass or polyester. Since its introduction in the 1950s GRP has become the material of choice for leisure craft because it is easier to clean and cheaper to maintain than other hull materials.

GRP lends itself to production-line techniques. Hulls and decks can be laid up by one company, using semi-skilled labour, and fitted out by another. Since the build quality is standardised, some builders have reduced woodworking, which is skilled, time-consuming and expensive, by dropping in GRP furniture modules with a little wood trim when fitting out the hull. There is nothing wrong with this in principle but some internal hull areas become inaccessible and there can be problems reaching seacocks and hull fittings for maintenance.

As more has become known about GRP, the very heavy lay-ups found in early boats have become progressively lighter. Modern isophthalic resins promise better water resistance than early resins and some boats are now laid up using epoxy rather than polyester resins with carbon fibre reinforcement. Some GRP hulls and decks, especially decks, may be of a sandwich construction where a layer of wood, usually end grain balsa, foam or paper honeycomb is sandwiched between two thin layers of GRP. This combines strength, lightness and rigidity but is not without its problems if the bond between the core and the GRP fails.

Another drawback with GRP is osmosis, where water penetrates the

This is a GRP production boat, typical of many thousands world-wide. Prices vary with age, size and build quality but somewhere there will be one that fits your budget.

gelcoat and collects in voids in the lay up, creating blisters on the hull and ultimately leading to delamination. Osmosis can be cured, but at a price. Otherwise GRP is a strong, easily-worked material, although if the hull is damaged, the more advanced laminates will require careful matching of materials to give a good repair.

BUILD STANDARDS

Claims that a production yacht meets Lloyd's A1 or any other standard does not mean that the boat was individually checked for compliance with the standard during its construction. This is done for one-offs but for production yachts these statements are based on checking a small, representative sample and then applying the results to an entire production run.

All yachts built in the EU must comply with the standards laid down in the Recreational Craft Directives.

There are few small ferro-cement hulls. Ferro boats were once popular with live-aboards and bluewater sailors but nowadays they have fallen out of favour and some insurance companies, concerned about build quality, are reluctant to provide cover. Many ferro hulls have plywood decks and sometimes the plywood is sheathed in an effort to avoid rot and to seal the leaks.

◆ FERRO-CEMENT

Ferro-cement has a surprisingly long history as a boat-building material. A steel shortage during World War 1 saw a short-lived project to build ferro-cement tugs and barges. Some examples survived into World War 2. Ferro-cement had a renaissance in the 1960s and 1970s when it was a very popular method for DIY yacht building as it gave the biggest possible hull for the least outlay.

An armature of steel rods and chicken wire mesh in the shape of the hull is plastered with cement. The quality of the finish depends on the skill of the plasterer and the life of the boat on how well the armature was treated against rust before plastering. Concrete is not completely water-proof. When moisture reaches the metal of an unprotected armature it rusts. Rust occupies more space than clean metal. Over time the layer of rust thickens to a level where the bond between the concrete and the armature fails. Cracks begin to appear and finally chunks of concrete fall off. This is called exfoliation. The first signs that it is happening are rust streaks running down the hull. These blemishes are sometimes explained by enthusiastic owners as 'cosmetic' rust. If you wish to buy a ferro-cement boat, then the extra cost of a professionally built hull is a better bet than self-build but even then it must be very carefully checked out by someone familiar with building these boats.

6 | Raising the cash

◆ BUYING NEW

Whether you are buying a new yacht direct from the yard or through an agent there is always scope for negotiation over the price.

Price reductions on new yachts will not be given if you do not ask and may be disguised as an upgrade in specification or having some of the charges that do not appear in the headline price knocked off the bill. Wrangling over money may appear a lot of trouble but a 3 or 4 per cent reduction on a five- or six-figure bill is always worth having. So don't be afraid to haggle, especially in the current economic climate.

◆ BUYING SECOND-HAND

Begin by checking that the asking price is within the going rate. In the USA there are a variety of publications, called Blue Books, listing typical prices for second-hand boats. Each Blue Book has its own system for calculating second-hand prices and their answers can vary by as much as 20 per cent.

BLUE BOOKS
The following are publishers of Blue Books:
ABOS Marine Blue Book Intertec Publishing PO Box 12901 Overland Park, KS 66282-2901
BUC Used Boat Price Guide BUC Research 1314 NE 17th Ct. Ft Lauderdale, FL 33305 (800) 327-6929
NADA Marine Appraisal Guide PO Box 7800 Costa Mesa, CA 92628 (800) 966-6232 www.nadaguides.com

To help close a deal, sellers will produce the higher figure to show what a good bargain you have driven and cynical bank managers prefer using the lower figure when working out how much they will loan against the boat's value. Wise buyers begin their negotiations around the lower figure.

In the UK and many other countries there is no Blue Book system. All you can do is check the asking price in the sailing press small ads. Or, if the boat is still in production, make some allowance for annual depreciation. Depreciation is greatest in the first three or four years and stops after a maximum of about ten years. Beyond that, variations in second-hand value depend entirely upon the boat's condition. Whether the boat is in good, fair or absolutely awful condition, work out your own figures for the cost of renovation.

Prices for the same boat can vary by region or country and it may be worth adjusting your prices to allow for this and widening your search.

◆ CAPITAL BUDGET

With luck, you ought to recover much of your capital when you come to sell, but if you intend to finance the purchase through a loan then the repayments must be included in your annual running cost figure.

Companies specialising in providing finance for the yachting market are often described as marine finance houses. They offer marine mortgages of about 50–80 per cent of the boat's value, probably based on the lowest valuation, for between five to ten years on a fixed rate.

To qualify for a marine mortgage it is normal for a yacht to be registered. In the UK this means the Part 1 Register and not the cheaper Small Ship Register. Putting a previously unregistered second-hand vessel on the Part 1 Register requires evidence of ownership covering the last five years. Part 1 Registration lasts for five years and the finance company can put the mortgage on the ship's papers, making it impossible to sell the boat without their agreement. Registration costs must be included in your budget.

In the USA, a marine mortgage is called a 'preferred' mortgage, and if a boat is registered with the Federal (as opposed to state) authorities, a preferred mortgage can appear on the documentation in exactly the same way as a marine mortgage in the UK.

When looking for a loan, what you want is a (low) fixed interest rate loan with no penalty for paying off the loan early. What you actually get can be very different. Lenders normally expect a down payment; the greater your deposit, the cheaper the loan.

If loan repayments take your annual budget beyond a sum that you can reasonably afford then consider looking for a cheaper, smaller boat. Alternatively, you could take advantage of the fact that the longer the term of the loan, the lower the monthly repayments, and extend the loan period to bring the monthly repayments down to an affordable level.

Take this option with caution. Longer loan periods mean a higher final bill. You could end up paying back twice or even three times the sum borrowed and if it is likely that you will sell within the first five years then financing the purchase of a yacht over ten or fifteen years is not good sense.

◆ REVENUE BUDGET

The revenue budget is the day-to-day running costs, including loan repayments if you have borrowed money to buy the boat, and once spent revenue costs, unlike capital expenditure, are not recoverable.

Annual running costs have more to do with a boat's size than its purchase price. In theory, for the first few years new boats ought to have lower running costs than older boats but this does not mean that they are maintenance free. Hulls still need cleaning and antifouling, brightwork requires varnishing, engines servicing and sails valeting. On older boats there needs to be a sensible rolling programme for replacing or upgrading equipment as it reaches the end of its useful working life.

Before you rush out and buy, work through the annual running costs by putting your best estimate of what you can afford to spend against each element. If your figures are wildly different from what you realistically will spend then scratch around until you have a satisfactory explanation for the discrepancy. When you have found it and corrected your figures what you

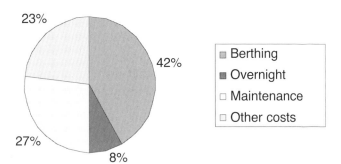

Breakdown of annual costs

now have is your best estimate of annual running costs and the question is, can you afford them? If not, you need to make savings.

An obvious start is a cheaper berth. Finding a cheaper berth brings serious savings. More time at anchor rather than in marinas during your summer cruise cuts costs as do money saving ploys during the annual refit.

Shopping around can produce lower insurance premiums but savings from these and items like personal equipment are minimal compared to those from berthing and maintenance.

Realistically, the maximum savings you can make on your annual revenue budget will not exceed 30–45 per cent of your initial budget. If this does not bring your expenditure into line with your pocket then you must consider downsizing. If you wish to race, this may mean racing dinghies instead of larger, more expensive club racers. If you cruise, then buy a smaller boat.

CALCULATING ANNUAL RUNNING COSTS

Berthing	Maintenance	Other costs
Annual berthing fees	Haul-out fees	Insurance
Overnight fees when cruising	Hidden haul-out extras such as jet washing the hull and renting a cradle when out of the water	Updating and replacing personal equipment
	Paints, varnishes, cleaning and painting materials	Travel to and from your home to your boat
	Servicing engine and other equipment such as stern bearings, hull, deck fittings, liferaft and EPIRBs	Club membership fees
	Replenishing stocks of spares including filters and fan belts	Licence fees and harbour/river authority charges
	Replacing and upgrading equipment that has reached the end of its useful working life	10–15% contingency fund

7 | Where to find your boat

There are thousands of second-hand boats of all shapes, sizes and pedigrees for sale, and with a little wishful thinking, they can all be made to sound the perfect boat for you. If you are not specific about what sort of boat you want then your search, like that for the Holy Grail, will be an interesting, colourful, costly but ultimately unsuccessful quest. Write down the specification of the sort of boat you are looking for and stick to it. It saves time, money, wasted effort and disappointment.

◆ WORD OF MOUTH

In your local sailing scene you may hear of a boat you know, like and consider suitable coming onto the market. If it meets your specification then this is probably the simplest, safest and surest way of buying a second-hand boat but check the boat and the deal on offer very carefully first. A deal going sour between mates is a great way of losing both a friendship and cash.

◆ YACHT CLUBS AND MARINAS

Yacht club notice boards always carry home-made ads for local boats. There is a good chance you will either know the boat, its owner or someone who does. Unravelling its previous history is simple. Walking

Yacht club notice boards are used by individuals rather than agents or brokers to advertise boats for sale.

round marinas and boatyards you may see the boat you want with a 'for sail' sign and contact number in the window.

◆ BOAT SALES

Occasionally, marinas and yards organise second-hand boat sales where brokers and boat owners with boats to sell can display their wares. Sometimes you will find special offers on the price or attractive finance deals to hurry you into a quick decision. Some of these events concentrate on a particular type, class or make of boat. If it does, and it is the sort of boat that you are interested in buying, then this is a good opportunity of seeing a lot of your type of boat together and acquiring a feel for the market. You do not need to buy on the day. Following up possible deals a day or two later may place you in a better bargaining position.

◆ YACHTING PRESS

Most yachting magazines contain a section of small ads for second-hand boats which are updated each time the magazine is published. Some magazines contain nothing but adverts for second-hand boats. Stick to magazines that cover your type of sailing.

◆ YACHT BROKERS

Yacht brokers have lists of boats they are selling on behalf of someone else. They advertise some of the boats on their current list for sale in yachting magazines which gives you a good idea of the type of boat they specialise in selling. If none of the boats currently on their books is what you want then they will use their contacts with other brokers to search for a suitable boat.

To encourage sales of new boats, many dealerships take an owner's present boat in part exchange. In this way they build up a stock of second-hand boats and combine selling new boats with a brokerage service for second-hand boats.

A broker's services should be free to buyers with the broker's fee being paid by the seller. It is important to select a broker who specialises in the sort of boat you wish to buy. This should be clear from their adverts and, if possible, use a local broker that you can speak to face to face. Ideally your broker will be a member of a professional body such as the Association of

Boats in marinas sometimes have 'For Sale' signs displayed (inset). Although these may look like private sales, they may in fact be handled by brokers. Some marinas insist that they or their nominated broker handle all sales of boats in the marina.

Brokers and Yacht Agents (ABYA) in the UK (www.abya.co.uk) or, in the USA, the Yacht Brokers Association of America (www.ybaa.org). There are also state associations such as the Florida Yacht Brokers Association (www.fyba.org), and the California Yacht Brokers Association (http://www.yachtcouncil.com/california-yacht-brokers-association.asp).

A good broker takes time to discover your sort of sailing and if inexperience or ill-informed ambition is leading you towards an unsuitable type of boat they gently guide you back onto the right track. Then, when you have found a suitable boat, they guide you through the purchasing process. They have one eye on repeat business. A poor broker, thinking only of his commission, begins asking how much you are prepared to pay and goes through his books looking for boats at the top end of, or even a little beyond, your budget whether they are suitable or not.

◆ THE INTERNET

Enter 'second-hand boat' in any internet search engine and you could face thousands of entries. Restrict choice by specifying:

1   Type of boat by class, manufacturer and age
2   Length of boat
3   Price range
4   Country/region where boat is based
5   Construction material: wood, GRP, aluminium, steel or ferro-concrete
6   Monohull, catamaran or trimaran
7   Rig

◆ BUYING ABROAD

Yachting magazines frequently carry adverts for yachts based in exotic locations and the internet opens up the entire world of second-hand boats.
Prices overseas sometimes appear extraordinarily cheap but there are pitfalls. How do you check whether the boat is as described? Is the boat debt
free? What flag is the boat currently sailing under? Where is it registered?
Is there a language problem which may lead to inconvenient misunder-
standings? Which country's laws apply to the sale? Do you appoint a local
agent to represent your interests? If so, how do you find one you can trust?
How many distant yachts can you afford to check out? How do you find
a trustworthy surveyor? If you buy a boat abroad then how do you bring it
home? Will there be import duties and taxes payable when you do? Does
the boat meet your national construction standards? Is there any realistic
scope for redress if you have been deliberately misled? The answers to these
questions vary from country to country and they all have cost implications
over and above the asking price of the boat. Only once you have checked
all this out and done your sums will you know if buying a boat abroad
brings you worthwhile savings.

When buying abroad, do not unquestioningly accept the seller's
unsupported word on any point. There may be no intention to deliberately
mislead but the effect is the same. He may, for example, not have heard of
your national construction standards or the EU's RCD directives and when
asked whether the boat complies with the regulations say 'Yes', assuming
standards in all countries are the same. Or claim his boat is registered, and
it is – but only with his local harbour authorities.

Whether purchasing at home or abroad there is a danger that the hunt
for the right boat becomes an end in itself. You keep looking for the ideal
because however close you have come to ticking all the boxes on your wish
list you know that the yacht for you is still out there . . . somewhere. Only
you can decide how far you go and how long you spend in your search.

8 | Is this boat suitable?

Once you have a list of boats that appear to meet your needs, you must weed out those that do not merit the time, effort and expense to travel and view them. Looking at boats is costly in both time and money and you wish to be sure both are well spent. The process begins by working through a detailed inventory, photographs of above and below decks and particulars of where she is berthed, sailed and wintered.

◆ THE INVENTORY

It is sometimes possible to download this information from adverts on the internet but these photos are often postage-stamp sized and at a resolution that makes detailed examination impossible. The inventory that goes out with the advert sometimes amounts to no more than four or five items or catch-all phrases like 'full instrumentation'. What you need are decent-quality photos, the make and age of everything in the sail wardrobe, full details of the sail-handling systems, engines, winches and deck hardware, electronics, autopilots, galley equipment, liferaft and a list of every item being sold with the boat.

It is a good idea to ask for this information even if you are buying a new boat, especially a 'sail-away' version. You may be surprised how little equipment 'sail-away' includes.

The inventory is also a clue as to the owner's type of sailing. A boat that has made bluewater cruises should have windvane self steering, wind or solar generators and heavy ground tackle. There should be dodgers and pramhoods to protect the crew when they are in the cockpit and a bimini or cockpit tent to make life more comfortable at anchor or in harbour. If these items are not on the inventory, have they been sold separately? A racing yacht should have a large inventory of sails. If not, why not?

The photographs are a pointer to her condition but use them with caution. Pictures may not lie but every photograph misleads if only because it is selective. Photograph the cabin of a small 20-footer from a dozen different viewpoints with a wide angle lens and it is easy to believe that you are looking at a multi-storey gin palace. Just as interesting as the pictures the seller is happy to provide are those areas that have not been photographed.

◆ WHERE IS THE BOAT BERTHED?

Where a boat is normally berthed helps you to decide how often she is sailed. If it is a three- or four-hour drive from the owner's home or place of work then claims of sailing two or three evenings a week, every week, are suspicious. Statements that the boat is sailed three or four thousand miles every season are questionable. A good cruising average is 100 miles in 24 hours. Most sailors are hard pushed to find time for a two-week cruise and half of that is spent in harbour. It would be exceptional to cover 1000 miles during the average summer cruise and claims of another two or three thousand miles sailing at weekends stretches credulity beyond breaking point.

If a boat is kept on a drying mooring then is it on sand or mud? If it is sand then during every tide there will be times she bumps with every passing wave until she is properly afloat or fully dried out. The bigger the wave, the greater the thump. Years of this thumping does the hull no good.

◆ WINTER LAYING UP

If her hull is GRP and every winter has been spent afloat then the possibility of osmosis is above average. A couple of days lift-out each year to scrub and antifoul does not leave a lot of time to give tender loving care to underwater fittings. How is the boat winterised? If the winter is spent ashore, is this in a yard or under cover?

◆ FIRST CONTACT

The first point of contact is usually a phone call. How you approach this discussion is a personal matter but remember it is a conversation, not an interrogation. Try to avoid asking one question after another but it may help to ask the same question at different times in slightly different ways. You have the common ground of sailing and questions can be slipped in as you talk about cruises you have both made and boats you have sailed.

An obvious starting point is to ask why the boat is up for sail. How long has the boat been on the market? Where is it lying? When did he buy the boat? Was it then second-hand or new? If second-hand then how many owners has the boat had? Is the seller buying a new boat? What sort and why? Is he giving up sailing?

◆ LEARNING ABOUT THE SELLER

Some important questions that need answers: What is the owner's experience of sailing? His usual sailing grounds? How long has the present owner owned the boat? How many boats has he owned? What sailing has he done in the last two seasons? What was his longest non-stop passage in this boat? What was his longest cruise? When and where to? How many were aboard? What was the worst weather he has sailed in? How did the boat behave?

◆ LEARNING ABOUT THE BOAT

Clarify any inconsistencies between what appears on the inventory and claims of sailing experience and maintenance regime. If it is a GRP boat ask about the condition of the gel coat. Has the hull been treated for osmosis? If a wooden boat is presently stored ashore how long has it been out of the water? Is it under cover? Salt water does not rot wood but rainwater does. Wooden boats left ashore and not under cover are likely to have problems with rot. If it is a steel boat how has the hull been treated? When was the hull last painted? With what kind of paint?

Where does he keep the boat during the winter? Ask what annual maintenance is carried out on:

1 Hull including deck, hatches, windows. Have any of the windows been replaced? Have they ever leaked? Seals on windows over ten years old are suspect.
2 Spars and rigging: when was the standing rigging last replaced? Remember that insurance companies do not like standing rigging much over ten years old.
3 Hardware such as winches, pumps, electrical wiring and control panels, galley and electronics. Instruments age quickly and finding spares can be a problem. For example, locating electronic charts in a suitable format for older chart plotters may be impossible. Parts for older equipment may be unobtainable.
4 Steering system.
5 Stern gland, propshaft and flexible coupling.
6 Engine and fuel system. What was the date of the last major overhaul?
7 Sails; when were they last valeted?
8 Batteries; batteries more than a couple of years old need replacing.

Who carries out this maintenance? If maintenance is done by a yard, can you see the receipts for the work? Major maintenance such as an engine overhaul ought to be supported by receipts. An engine overhaul includes work on the cylinder head, valves, injectors, sea-water pump, fresh-water pump, oil pump, fuel pump, exhaust system, drive system and all senders and sensors like those for oil pressure and water temperature. You need to see a bill detailing the work, not a letterhead with a single, solitary figure for the entire job.

Have there been any modifications? If so, what are they and who carried them out? Has the boat ever grounded? If so, when, where and what was the outcome? Has there been any major damage? If so, what, how was it caused and who repaired it?

Sellers have an understandable and natural tendency to gloss over defects, especially faults that may scare buyers. Minor defects are another matter. Boats of the same class of a similar age all suffer from much the same problems and claims that any boat is free of faults are too good to be true.

Look for consistency within the answers and with the information you already have. Some contradictions may be obvious, others less so. A boat that has passed through several owners with none holding onto it for more than a season may have a defect, not immediately apparent to new owners but which is sufficiently serious for folk to cut their losses and run when they do find it.

◆ DEALING WITH BROKERS

Brokers may be reluctant to put you in direct contact with the seller. They may worry that you intend to cut them, and their commission, out of the loop or that the owner, less skilled in the art of selling, may say something that scares you off. If this is the case then explain that you are considering taking a look at the boat but that you have some questions you would like answered first so you do not make a long journey only to discover that the boat is obviously unsuitable for your needs. If the broker insists they have the answers (it is very unlikely he has the detail you need) then ask for his answers in writing, adding that if he is aware of any information which even distantly suggests that the boat is not exactly as claimed then this should be included.

9 | DIY yacht survey

◆ HULL AND DECK SURVEY

Having sorted the wheat from the chaff there will be a handful of boats on your list of possible purchases. The next step is deciding which boat on this list is best for you. This decision needs to be based on a survey but before commissioning a surveyor, take a look at the boat yourself. Time spent in reconnaissance is seldom wasted.

Any worthwhile inspection lasts several hours so even if a couple of boats are situated close together do not plan on visiting more than one boat a day. Take overalls, gloves, a flashlight, a tape measure, ruler, camera, spare batteries for both camera and flashlight, a bradawl or sharp penknife, mirror, notepad, pencil and copies of the inventory and photographs that the owner provided. The mirror is to peer into awkward corners and the bradawl is to poke suspicious-looking timber. No boat owner will like you doing this so use it discreetly.

If the owner or broker insists on staying with you once he has opened up the boat then they may offer some explanation or comment every time you make a note or take a photograph. Be non-committal and try not to become involved in any discussion on the points raised but do make a note of his remarks. They may come in useful later when negotiating over the price.

A wise seller has the boat looking as pretty as possible. If it is out of the water, the hull should have been power-washed. Below the waterline there should be new antifouling or, at the very least, any patches of bare hull painted over. The topsides should have been cleaned and polished. Below decks should have had a deep spring clean and lockers emptied of clutter and cleaned to give the impression of a spacious interior with lots of living room. The bilge, if not newly painted (a warning sign in its own right), should be sparkling bright without an oil smear or tide line in sight. In short, everything should have been done so that your first impression is, 'Wow, this is a great-looking boat!' and, so the seller hopes, this thought will blind you to any defects it may have. Your job is to look beyond the shine.

A TYPICAL CONDITION SURVEY

A typical condition survey covers the following points. Use it as a guide for your inspection.

1 Anchors and anchor rode

2 Batteries

3 Bilge pumps, manual and powered

4 Cathodic protection

5 Chain plates

6 Deck, coachroof and superstructure

7 Deck fittings including cleats, blocks, sail tracks, fairleads, jammers, halyard organisers etc

8 Electrical installation, including power generation

9 Engine[1] and engine controls

10 Engine instrumentation

11 Firefighting equipment

12 Fresh-water installations

13 Fuel tanks, filters and fuel lines

14 Galley

15 Guardrails and stanchions

16 Heads

17 Hull[2], keel and rudder/s

18 Internal hull structures, bulkheads, framing, fastenings, furniture etc

19 Lifesaving equipment

20 LPG[3] storage and pipework

21 Mast, boom, other spars and rigging

22 Navigation area

23 Navigation instruments

24 Navigation lights

25 Propshaft and stern gear

26   Sails, dodgers, pramhoods and cockpit awnings

27   Skin fittings and seacocks

28   Steering gear

29   Winches including anchor winches

30   Windows and hatches

1 The engine and its controls normally receive no more than a visual check. The engine checklist in Chapter 10 probably covers more ground than the sort of check the average surveyor carries but it is not as good as that by a professional marine engineer. If you are concerned about the condition of the engine, have it surveyed by a professional engineer.

2 Steel and aluminium hulls are sometimes checked using ultrasound but this often incurs an extra charge.

It is standard practice to remove small areas of antifouling on GRP hulls to check the condition of the hull underneath and take moisture readings.

Wooden hulls may be probed to check for rot. If the owner agrees, and if you are prepared to pay for the work, some fastenings may be removed to check their condition.

It may be necessary, on hulls of all types, to open up some otherwise inaccessible areas where water may gather to check for water damage.

3 In the UK, LPG installations can only be signed off by a registered CORGI gas engineer.

The hull

Look along the hull from as many angles as possible. Does the gel coat look chalky even though it has been polished for your visit? If a dull or chalky-looking gel coat cannot be restored to gleaming brilliance with a light rubbing compound, then the hull needs painting.

If there has been hull damage, a good, professional repair should be invisible but if there is a blemish or deformity in the hull's otherwise smooth curve it may be a sign of a less than competent repair.

GRP does not like sharp angles so if you see one, for example where the hull meets the transom, look to see if patches of gel coat have broken away to reveal voids underneath. Check for stress cracking in the gel coat in and around the chain plates and deck fittings such as the bow roller.

Imagine the boat coming alongside a pontoon or jetty and think of where the hull would bump if the manoeuvre went badly. Once you have worked this out, check port and starboard for any signs of the topsides having been given a good thwack. If there is a wooden rubbing strip, check it for damage or to see if a new length has been scarfed in. Examine the bow to see if it has had a run-in with a pontoon.

It is obvious that this yacht has fallen onto its side and damaged its hull. A little more sanding and a couple of coats of paint and you would have to look very closely for the shadows and slight imperfections in the curve of the hull that would suggest there might have been damage. Always ask if there have been any repairs made to the boat.

If the boat is out of the water, check the keel for bumps or dents which suggest a close encounter with something hard. Are there signs of rust weeping from where the keel joins the hull? If so, then at the very least, the keel needs to come off and be cleaned up before being replaced. New keel bolts may also be required.

Check the hull for osmosis. Small bubbles and blisters are the most obvious sign and most common below the waterline. Osmosis is not fatal and can be cured but the remedy is costly.

Has the hull been painted? If so, with what type of paint and when? Was it painted above *and* below the waterline? Two or three coats of epoxy paint below the waterline reduces the risk of osmosis.

The deck

On GRP boats, decks are often cored. This construction offers lightness with rigidity but, as in any sandwich, the filling does not take kindly to being squeezed. Where a fitting is bolted through the deck, the balsa wood, foam or paper honeycomb core should have been cut away, replaced by solid GRP and then protected by a large backing pad. This is a time-consuming and expensive task. The temptation for builders to cut corners and not cut out the core is often irresistible. Leaving the core in place and then through-bolting deck fittings almost certainly guarantees water penetration into the core.

Cored laminate construction is a complex topic. Curves mean that when foam or balsa wood is used it must be in the form of small squares stuck onto scrim so that it follows the curve. As it does so, each square hinges open a little and if these gaps are not filled with resin when the GRP skin is laid up, they can later fill with water.

Every hole in a cored deck is a route for water to reach the core. If it does, then the core slowly becomes soggier and spongier and the deck loses both its strength and rigidity. Eventually the core parts company with the GRP skin and structural integrity disappears. This is most likely to happen around deck hardware. Tap the deck near all deck hardware with the handle of the bradawl. If a sharp tap becomes a dull thud there is every chance you have found some delamination. Bumps or wrinkles, sometimes called *crocodiling* or *aligatoring* because of the appearance, in these same areas are signs that delamination is almost certain.

On wooden-hulled boats, leaks are a fact of life since the wood shrinks or swells according to the weather. Sometimes a teak deck, real or faux, is laid over a GRP deck to improve its appearance. If the deck is not properly supported it will flex but it is possible that the teak and GRP flex at different rates. The difference need not be much, just enough to affect the join between the hull and the teak. Water leaking through the teak can travel some distance before entering the hull, making the source of the leak difficult to find.

Some steel and ferro-cement hulls have plywood decks and superstructures. Water can enter the plywood along its end joints causing it to delaminate and rot. This may be concealed under a coat of paint. Gentle prodding with the bradawl at the more obvious joints and anywhere water could accumulate may help find the rot. If the owner is unhappy at you prodding his deck, try tapping with the handle of the bradawl and listen for a dull thud.

Hull deck join

There are a variety of hull to deck joins and each has a clan of variants. The joint stiffens the hull and contributes to its structural strength. A poor join

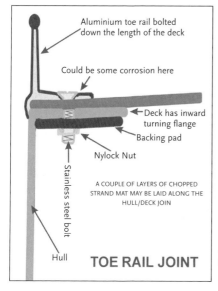

Aluminium toe rail bolted down the length of the deck

Could be some corrosion here

Deck has inward turning flange

Backing pad

Nylock Nut

A COUPLE OF LAYERS OF CHOPPED STRAND MAT MAY BE LAID ALONG THE HULL/DECK JOIN

Stainless steel bolt

Hull

TOE RAIL JOINT

can be a source of weakness and everlasting leaks.

The 'cocoa tin' system is easily the most common. The weakness of this joint is that it fits where it touches and the resulting gaps are filled with bodge. This is a mixture of cheap resin, hardener and floor sweepings. It ought to be scraped out and replaced with a decent structural adhesive.

Other joints include the toe rail clamp which uses an aluminium toe rail that comes ready pierced with scuppers for blocks and mooring lines.

Stemhead fittings

A stemhead fitting often doubles as a bow roller for the anchor rode and the attachment point for the forestay. In both roles it is subjected to high loadings and the fitting needs to be robustly constructed and attached to

This is a good example of a typical stemhead fitting. It is bolted to the deck and the hull. Unfortunately the tang bolting it to the hull bridges, rather than follows, the profile of the hull-deck joint and the resulting gap means that it is likely to leak. It is also multi-purpose, being a bow roller, and provides attachment points for the forestay, a downhaul and the pulpit. The outer line of bolts is too close to the hull to have any backing washers and the excess sealant suggests that it leaks.

Above left: This is a stemhead fitting for a motorboat as it is not designed to take the loads imposed by a forestay. It is made of aluminium and the bolts and shackle for the forestay and downhaul will saw their way through the aluminium. Despite an excess of sealant there are gaps between the fitting and the deck; where there are gaps there will be movement.

Above right: This small area of the foredeck is home to the forelegs of the pulpit, a cleat (but no fairleads) for the bow warp, and an eyebolt for the forestay which is not even lying parallel with the deck.

the hull and deck in such a way that the loadings are spread over as wide an area as possible. Look carefully for deformities in the stemhead fitting, stress cracks in the deck, an excess of sealant around the fitting and even rust marks round the bolts.

All too often, yards rely on penny washers to spread load and some yachts are famous for leaky stemhead fittings. Checking how the stemhead fitting is attached normally involves lying on your back in the forepeak and working at arm's length by touch and mirrors.

Sometimes manufacturers 'encapsulate' nuts of through-bolted deck fittings by covering them in a layer of chopped strand mat. If you want to upgrade or replace the stemhead fitting then the mat has to be chiselled off (working by touch) before a spanner can be used. Sometimes there is no room for a spanner and it is necessary to drill the head off the bolts and knock them through. It is not surprising that stemhead fittings come low on the maintenance totem and people live with its leaks.

Grabrails
Grabrails are to enable you to hang on for dear life while the boat is thrown onto its beam ends and waves threaten to wash you overboard. You can even clip your lifeline to them and stay attached to the boat should you

Above left: This is probably the cheapest form of grabrail and you get what you pay for. Would you trust your life to a half inch strip of wood and a couple of brass screws driven into GRP? Besides being dangerous, it also leaks.
Above right: This is a better form of grabrail if it is through-bolted to the deck. More usually it is attached by wood screws through the deck into the wood. It will leak, though, and water trapped between the grabrail and deck encourages the wood to rot and the screws to pull out. The cost of replacing poor grabrails is an additional negotiating point.

ever lose your grip. However, many grabrails are flimsy strips of wood that are so poorly attached to the coachroof that they would either break or pull out under a severe loading.

Deck fittings
Check that all deck fittings are securely attached and do not show signs of leaking. Check that the pulleys on all blocks run smoothly. Are there sufficient cleats in the right place and of the right size? Given the size of some cleats it seems that some manufacturers assume that yachtsmen use string or fishing line to moor their boats. Are there fairleads to protect the hull where lines leave the boat? Are there cleats midships port and starboard for springs? How is the anchor chain secured?

If there are faults with the deck fittings they were probably made when the boat was built but pointing out the need to upgrade is a useful negotiating tactic when discussing the price.

Chain plates
Chain plates have a hard life spent keeping the mast upright. The loading on chain plates varies with the wind strength and sea state. Unless properly supported, a chain plate waggles to and fro and up and down and can come loose. This not only weakens the entire arrangement but allows water to enter the hull. A sure sign that this is happening is some deformity in the chain plate or one of its components, or applications of sealant where it is attached to the deck or the hull.

The very considerable loads that chain plates carry should be spread

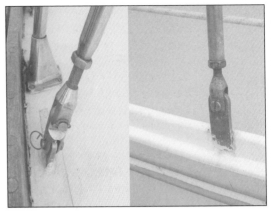

This type of chain plate is a very common form found on yachts up to 35ft (10m) LOA. A metal tang, bolted to a wooden backing pad, sticks up through the edge of the hull while the backing pad is glassed into the hull. It is guaranteed to leak, regardless of how much sealant is used. The only solution is to replace them with a better design.

over as great an area of the hull and deck as possible. To do this they should be tied into a bulkhead or to some structural member of the hull. It is surprising how often this basic rule, which most sailors know, is ignored. Occasionally (mostly on racing yachts) bulkheads are cored to save weight, even those with chain plates attached. This is fine provided that subsequent water penetration has not destroyed the bulkhead's structural integrity.

On some boats the shrouds are fixed to the coachroof, which would be acceptable if they were then tied into a bulkhead or beam that would take the load into the hull. Usually they are not. Sometimes they are even bolted

Left: The glassfibre covering this backing pad has been cut away to reveal the pad and to allow trapped water to drain away. The staining from this is obvious. It is impossible to attach this form of chain plate securely to the hull. Chain plates must be properly tied into features like bulkheads or ribs that spread the load throughout the hull. Always check chain plates for leaks. Redesigning and replacing chain plates is a major job.

Far left: This is another common form of chain plate. It should be attached to a bulkhead or a beam which takes the load down into the hull but in this case it is simply through-bolted onto the side deck and the lavish applications of sealant warns of chronic leaks.

on immediately above or below a window opening which not only makes it impossible to tie them into any structural member but more or less guarantees that the window will leak.

Backstays often end in a bridle attached to the transom by small stainless steel triangular-shaped plates on, or very close to, the hull deck join. The loading is carried entirely by the backing pads to the bolts holding these plates. These are usually no more than penny washers and salesmen have been known to reassure prospective customers that this is acceptable because the loading on the bolts is in 'sheer'.

Poorly fitted or badly designed chain plates are design faults and expensive to put right. If your dream boat has them then you must either live with them, or redesign and replace the chain plates. If you find evidence of water penetration through the chain plates then you can ask the vendor to contribute towards the cost of remedial work.

Windows

Windows in hulls and coachroofs flex and twist and, as they do, the hole cut out to accommodate the window changes shape. This breaks the seal

Here is a typical aluminium window frame with a toughened glass window and rubber seals that have reached the end of their useful life. It is possible, on older boats, that proprietary frames like these are no longer manufactured and new seals are not available. The only solution is a new window. This gives another negotiating point when discussing the price.

between the window frame and the coachroof or hull. Once the seal is broken, water can enter. Preventing this happening has always taxed the ingenuity of boatbuilders.

Most solutions rely on rubber seals with or without an aluminium frame. Another popular answer is a Perspex® window, cut to shape and attached directly to the coachroof. If this is the case, check that it is held in place by bolts, not screws, and that the holes drilled for the bolts have not caused stress cracking in the Perspex®. Stress cracking is normally the result of drilling holes with a blunt bit. The danger it brings is that a sharp bang can shatter the window. This could be interesting if you are in heavy weather at the time.

Old, crazed or cracked plastic windows, corroding frames and aged rubber seals need replacing and are useful points to raise when negotiating the price.

Stanchions

Designed to hold up guard wires, stanchions become levers when they are used to fend boats off, pull yourself aboard or as cleats for mooring lines. The forces that this mistreatment applies far exceed those that any stanchion is designed to take. Yet this abuse happens and will continue to happen as surely as night follows day. The only answer is better and stronger stanchions.

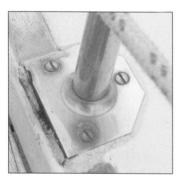 

Above left: The fact that this stanchion leaks is the least of your worries. Would you trust your life to this arrangement? It is of such flimsy metal (2mm stainless steel) and so poor a design that the only cure is to throw it away and replace it with a substantial, properly-designed unit.

Above right: Stainless steel wire with aluminium uprights is not a good combination. These uprights are not repairable.

Stanchions usually come in two parts: a base with a socket that is fixed to the deck and an aluminium or stainless steel tube 24–30in (60–76cm) long which fits into the socket and is drilled to take the guard wires.

Failure of the tube is rare and when it happens it is usually just above where it leaves the socket. Most of the loading is taken by the base, levering it away from the deck, allowing water in and sometimes weakening the fixing to the point of failure. Stanchions are normally located on the very edge of the deck which means there is almost no space at all for decent backing pads. Repairs involve working in impossibly cramped spaces.

Problems with stanchions are revealed by kinks in the tube, deformed bases and applications of sealant around the base.

Check the guardrail wire. Bare wire has been known to saw its way through stanchions and plastic coated wire can rot unseen.

Boats which have narrow side decks going forward from the cockpit can mean climbing outside the guardrails until you reach the foredeck, where you climb back over them to stand on the foredeck. In a seaway this can be dangerous and raises questions about the value of having guardrails.

Navigation lights

If there is only a masthead tricolour and the mast is stepped then all you can do is switch it on and check that it lights up unless you are prepared to climb the mast. Leisure craft navigation lights are notorious for being almost invisible to other shipping. It does not help that some boat owners use a bulb lower than the recommended wattage or that over the years the lens has grown a white patina of closely packed fine cracks. Unless it is possible to buy new lenses, the only solution is a new light.

UV light degrades plastic. It has given this lens so many fine cracks that it looks like it is covered in a white dust. It needs either a new lens, or if that is not available, the light must be replaced – another negotiating point when discussing the price.

The cockpit

Stand in the cockpit and imagine tacking the boat in a blow. Is there enough room for the crew to work and move around without falling over each other? Are the sheets and winches easily accessible? Can the winches be used without their handles thumping someone in the back? Are there strong points for safety harnesses? Are there enough of these strong points so that lifelines do not become a tangled mess? Can the helmsman reach the lifebuoys without leaving the tiller or wheel unattended?

Cockpit instruments

Fitting cockpit instruments so that they can be easily seen by the helmsman is always a challenge on a small boat. It is hardly fair to class their position as a defect but it is worth making a note if only because you might wish to change them if you buy the boat.

Cockpit lockers

Can the cockpit lockers be secured at sea? If the boat is knocked down you do not wish the lockers to open and throw their contents overboard as water rushes in. Do they have decent-sized gutters to drain away the water that always slops around cockpits? Hatches to cockpit lockers double as seats. Is there some arrangement to prevent the crew sitting in the puddles that collect when the boat heels?

Cockpit drains

If there is a self-draining cockpit, are the drains of a decent size? Do their hoses cross and lead to seacocks? If there is not a self-draining cockpit, what arrangement has been make to clear the cockpit of water? How easy is it to clear the water from the cockpit?

Cockpit hatches

The main hatch should be above a bridgedeck and have a decent-sized sill to prevent water running into the main cabin. If this hatch is closed by washboards, examine how the rebate they fit into is attached to the boat.

Sometimes this is a moulding in the GRP – which is fine. Other times it is nothing more than a length of channelled wood held in place by two or three screws into GRP. Think about the effect that a wave would have if it hits this arrangement and when you realise how vulnerable it is to a sudden bang, consider how it can be upgraded.

Hatches are often let into the cockpit sole to give access to the engine

On this hatch the washboards fit into a moulding in the hull. This is good. On some boats they fit into a grooved length of wood held in place by a couple of screws, which is poor design and needs upgrading.

or propshaft. Are these hatches watertight? How are they secured? Would gravity let them fall open in a knockdown?

Upgrading hatches and washboards is not difficult but costs money and is another point to remember when negotiating the price.

Mast and rigging

If the mast has been unstepped and stored ashore you can take a close look. Otherwise you will need a pair of binoculars. You are looking for any deformities or signs of cracking, especially around fittings like winches,

Deck-stepped masts fit into traditional tabernacles or onto T and U-shaped channels. The tabernacle or channel must be on the centre line of the boat, bolted to the deck, and have some means of carrying the loads that the mast imposes down to the keel. If the deck is cored it is important that the core around the mast has been cut out and replaced with GRP.

cleats, spinnaker pole attachments and, most importantly, spreaders.

Check the boom, especially where the mainsheet is attached and at the gooseneck. A single involuntary gybe can wreak havoc on the strongest of goosenecks. Make sure whatever mainsail reefing arrangement is used – in-mast, in-boom, slab, traditional or single line jiffy reefing – works.

If there is a spinnaker pole, check it is the right size and that the end fittings have not seized up.

Check the standing rigging for any broken wires and ask its age. Rigging approaching the end of its useful working life needs replacing, doubly so if it is stainless steel rod. Rod rigging can develop hairline cracks that are invisible unless checked electronically; it looks perfect until it fails.

Check the bottle screws (turnbuckles) are not bent or distorted in any way. Some owners wrap bottle screws in electrician's tape which traps water and encourages corrosion. Confirm that the bottle screws are held together by clevis pins and not nuts and bolts. A 5mm nut has about the same strength as a 3mm clevis pin.

Check that the running rigging is not frayed and is the right size and length for the job.

Few yachts nowadays hank on foresails. Racing yachts tend to have foils and cruising yachts use a headsail roller reefing system. Check that the foil on both these systems is not bent through misuse and that it works. On reefing systems confirm that the line feeds neatly onto the drum without any snagging and that it is easily accessible in the cockpit. On small boats, it should be somewhere near the centre line. If it is on a cockpit coaming then on one tack it could be underwater.

Sails

If sails feel thin and are frayed round the head, tack or clew or if there are lines of broken or missing stitching then they are due for replacement. If a headsail has a sacrificial strip to protect it from UV, give the strip a good tug. If it begins to rip, stop. It needs replacing, which can cost up to 20–25 per cent of a new sail. Are the battens in the mainsail mix and match? If so it suggests that they have a habit of breaking or popping out of their pocket at sea. It is simple to stitch the pockets shut but if battens are breaking then new, stronger versions are needed.

Deck hatches

Every hatch is a possible leak so check that it seals. Excessive amounts of self-adhesive neoprene foam around hatches hints at problems. Can a strongback be fitted to make sure a hatch stays shut in heavy weather? If it is a hinged hatch the hinge should be on its forward edge so that there is less chance of a wave getting underneath and opening it. How easy is it to replace the seals?

If a hatch slides shut does it do so smoothly? What is the sliding arrangement? Is there a cover to prevent water coming below?

Ground tackle

Owners may spend tens of thousands of pounds on a boat but are reluctant to spend a couple of hundred on a decent anchor and anchor rode. Check the anchor is the right size for the boat, and that the anchor rode matches the anchor. Is it in good condition and sufficient to anchor in 15–20 metres of water?

If the chain locker has a hawse pipe, check that the anchor rode runs out easily. Some owners begin their anchor rode with a length of heavy chain, then, to save weight, shackle on lighter chain. It has been known for the shackle to be bigger than both chains and catch on the hawse pipe before the anchor reaches the bottom. This is embarrassing. The only way to check that this does not happen is to pull all the anchor rode out, and then feed it all back. The solution can be as simple as replacing the shackle with a proper chain link. If not, you need a new anchor rode.

Does the anchor locker drain outboard? Are the drains clear or has the chain been rusting in a puddle of water?

Steering system

Go from hard a-port to hard a-starboard several times. Does it go over smoothly or are there hesitations or bumps and bangs of unknown origin indicating stretched steering cables, worn bearings, mechanical damage or sloppy hydraulics? If the boat is out of the water, push the rudder from side to side while someone else holds the tiller or the wheel steady. If the rudder moves then the pintles (if transom hung) or bearings are worn and ought to be replaced. If it is a wooden laminated tiller, is it in good condition?

Once you have finished checking above decks it is time to take a look below.

◆ BELOW DECK SURVEY

When you first step into the cabin, stop. Absorb the atmosphere. Below decks should be as bright as a new pin but what is the scent of the air freshener camouflaging? It could be the odour from the heads but it might be the stink of mildew, damp and rot.

Now, imagine this spacious, stable, horizontal interior after a couple of days of heavy weather. Those off watch flop on the settees, which have lee cloths up so there is nowhere for anyone to sit. In the forecabin, damp oilies spill out of the wet locker, gear falls out of lockers, drawers fly open, the cook has spent an hour heating a couple of cans of soup and then dropped the pot on the cabin sole. The navigator cannot stay in his seat long enough to plot a fix.

A lack of handholds turns the cabin into a torture chamber and the cabin table exacts a heavy toll of bruises on every passerby. The steps from the main hatch into the cabin have a nasty habit of throwing people into or out of the cabin as the whim takes them. The crew have grown tired and irritable and wish to sit under a tree.

The point when everlasting discomfort and inconvenience ceases to be a challenge and becomes dangerously unacceptable is down to personal judgement. What some regard as part of the fun of cruising others see as a pain in the neck. Exactly when this happens varies from boat to boat. Give some thought as to where the line is on this boat rather than simply accepting what you see on a warm day on a boat on dry land.

Cabin sole

Begin your inspection with the cabin sole. Is it non slip? A wooden veneer looks pretty but it can have the coefficient of friction of an ice rink. Carpeting is another homely touch but where is the carpet stowed at sea? Or do you live with a smelly, damp carpet rotting the cabin sole?

Does the cabin sole flex as you walk around? Flexing hints at inadequate materials and insufficient support. The flatter hulls of modern yachts makes a little water in the bilge go a long way. At modest angles of heel, water laps round the plywood of the cabin sole. Soaked in water long enough, all plywood delaminates. Lift the cabin sole and look carefully for any signs of this happening. It may explain the flex.

If it does not, then check what holds the cabin sole up. Often it is untreated softwood battens screwed into the front edge of a bunk, or on larger craft, a grid of battens spanning the boat. Softwoods do not like water, particularly around the screw holes and end grains where water wicks along the wood.

If the battens are in good condition then the rule is the thinner the wood of the cabin sole then the more closely spaced are the battens holding it up.

The floors

The floors run athwartships and hold the keel together. Are they still firmly attached to the hull? If there is a tide mark in the bilge, then there has been water round the floors which has encouraged them to delaminate. It is not a big job to re-attach them but it probably requires running a dehumidifier for a couple of days to make sure that the wood that forms the floors is dry and ready to be glassed in.

Keel bolts

If there are keel bolts, check their condition and how they spread the load of carrying the keel around the hull. Penny washers are not an acceptable answer.

If the keel is encapsulated, what material is used for ballast? If it is iron then is it protected from water in the bilge? Rusty ballast occupies more space than clean iron and can weaken the encapsulation.

If there is a lifting keel and the boat is afloat, lower and raise the keel a couple of times. Is it easy to use? Does it work smoothly? Are the wires, rods or whatever does the work in good condition? If electric motors or hydraulics are involved, is there a manual back-up in case of failure? If the lifting mechanism fails, is there anything to stop the keel falling out? If the box is made of steel or wood, what precautions have been taken to stop it rotting from the inside out? If any part of the box is a component of some other structure such as a fuel tank what would be the consequences of a leak? It has been known for a keel box to be one side of a fuel tank, it leaked, and the first the owner knew of it was a bilge full of diesel.

Doors, lockers and drawers

Do all cabin doors open and close easily? They almost certainly did when the boat first left the yard but dropping off a wave can cause a hull to flex and twist; although the doors remain square, the doorways do not. In minor cases they need a good tug to open and a kick to close. In severe cases they will not close or if closed do not open. The ends of your ruler are square. If the doors are stiff then use the ends of your ruler to check the door frame is square. If not, then there is a serious problem and there is also the possibility the twisting has loosened or detached structural bulkheads from the hull. Reluctant doors are a reminder to look at every bulkhead.

Lockers with doors need good catches if they are not to open every time the boat bounces. Give all locker doors a light pull and if a locker opens there might be a problem. Close it. Now thump the door or its frame. If it opens there is a problem. The owner may be aghast at this behaviour but if you are thrown against a locker in a seaway you do not wish to be covered in its contents.

Lockers under side decks are the last resting place for water leaking through deck fittings. Check inside lockers for any staining. Black stains under varnish are a reliable indicator of water damage, as are rust marks round bolts.

Drawers sometimes swell and refuse to open. This does not often happen to drawers made of plywood as ply is a fairly stable material but solid wood drawers swelling or shrinking, depending on the amount of moisture in the air, have been known to jam. It is a sad example of an upmarket feature which can backfire and one you must live with.

Cushions

If you intend to sleep aboard then bunk cushions need to be a minimum of four inches thick, six is better and conformal foam better still. Foam cushions are expensive and many boats settle for three- or even two-inch thick cushions.

If the cushions have cloth rather than vinyl covers, check them for water staining. Water leaking into lockers continues down the hull until it reaches a bunk, where it flows below the cushion into the under bunk locker and so to the bilge. Cloth-covered bunk cushions look homely but they allow this water to soak into the foam and leave tide marks along the bottom edge and underneath the cushion. The smell of constantly damp foam is unmistakable and sleeping on a damp foam mattress is not good for your health.

Salt absorbs water from the air. Once soaked with sea water, cushions never dry out properly. How easy is it to remove the cushion covers so that the salt can be rinsed out of the foam? The zips may be made of plastic but the slide that pulls a zip together is normally made of alloy which corrodes and locks into position. If the cushions are in poor shape the answers are new, much bigger zips, new covers or new cushions, another negotiating point when discussing the price.

Deck lining

Deck linings conceal untidy wiring runs and the nuts and backing pads of deck fittings, giving the deckhead a civilised, uncluttered appearance. They guard against condensation but also hide leaks. Water has been known to follow wiring runs under the deck liner and collect in light fittings. It also puddles inside the lining and stains it. A saggy, stained headliner showing signs of being inexpertly removed and replaced speaks of these problems.

Domestic lights

Domestic lights are often positioned with more regard to short wiring runs than practicality. There is nothing worse than trying to read a book or chart with the light shining in your eyes; or that every cabin light blinds those in the cockpit. Is there a red light to protect night vision? What arrangements have been made for lighting the engine compartment? Or do you hold a torch between your teeth as you scrabble to change an oil filter?

Lights mounted on deckheads spread their light around better than lights mounted on bulkheads. More localised light for reading in your bunk or working on the chart table can be provided by small downward-shining lamps which will lessen the risk of blinding those on deck.

Lights mounted on bulkheads often shine directly into your eyes or straight into the cockpit. This is not a fatal flaw. Relocating lights is not a big job but it is another useful negotiating point. Also, check how easy it is to replace the bulb in a light. This type needs a screwdriver.

Heads

Do the heads give their occupants privacy? Does the pump to empty them work or does water spray out of the pump as you flush? This is not a serious fault but new seals are surprisingly expensive. Is there a holding tank? More and more cruising areas prohibit raw sewage from being pumped overboard. If there is not a holding tank you may need to fit one. Do the toilet's seacocks and valves work? Are they easily accessible for maintenance?

Fresh-water supply

If fresh water is hand-pumped to a sink does the pump work? Does it leak? If it is a foot pump, can you brace yourself and still have both hands free if you are using it in a seaway? If it relies on an electric pump, is there a back-up system if it fails? Automatic pumps means high water consumption. Is the tank large enough to hold enough water for a typical passage? Is there more than one tank? Where are they?

Water is heavy. A 40 gallon (181 litres) under-bunk tank in the fore-peak, a common location on today's yachts with their shallow bilges, is the equivalent of parking two or three crew members on the foredeck. Worse, when a yacht heels, the water in a part-full tank moves downhill and puts its weight in the wrong place.

Is the tank accessible for cleaning? Is the piping of food quality standard? Are the joints in the system secure and not showing any signs of leaking? Are there in-line water filters? How old are they? Are they easy to source and replace?

Are the tanks made of rigid material, like GRP, or bladder tanks fitted into lockers and odd corners? Water slops around in all tanks, even bladder tanks, and if no precautions have been taken to protect against chafe then, at some point, bladder tanks leak. It may take some years for this to happen but it will.

Gas supply

Most boats cook on gas. Gas bottles should be securely stowed in a sealed locker with an outboard drain which exits the hull below the bottles but far enough above the waterline so that water cannot siphon back when heeled. The pipework should be of a recognised standard and installed by a qualified engineer. Blowback arresters, leak detectors and gas alarms are a sign that the risk of using gas is taken seriously.

Living below

A caravan-type layout is fine if life below decks is confined to marinas and anchorages but on overnight and extended passages it is important that the cabin is suited to life afloat and is comfortable and stress free. Can you sit on the settee berths when the boat is heeled? Are there decent leecloths so you can sleep without falling out of bed? Are the galley and navigation areas laid out so you can safely work in them when heeled up to 20° in a vigorous seaway? Are the ready-to-use lockers easily reached? Is there somewhere to stow wet oilies?

ENGINE CHECKLIST

A well maintained engine should look clean and tidy. There should be no signs of oil leaking into the bilges or around gaskets, pipes and hoses. Engine checks are:

1   Take out the dipstick and examine the oil on it.
    - Normally it will be black or a very dark brown. If it has been changed recently then it should look clear and clean. If this is the case ask when it was changed and how long the engine has run since then. Take a look at the oil filter. It is usual to change the filter when you change the oil. Clean oil with an old filter is suspect.
    - The oil should run down the dipstick easily.
    - Thick, treacle-like oil suggests a lack of engine maintenance.
    - If it looks milky, this is a sign of a water leak within the engine.

2   A chalky residue on the engine is a sign that it is running hot.

3   If it is a petrol engine, pull out a spark plug. If it is in poor condition, this could point towards a lack of maintenance.

4   What is the condition of the engine mounts? Engine mounts rely on the bond between rubber and metal to absorb vibration. They are suspect and need replacing if the mounts are rusty.

5   Check all the drive belts. Are they slack, worn, cracked or in any way degraded? If so, this points to poor maintenance.

6   Check the fuel lines for leaks.

7   Check the oil in the gearbox. This should be absolutely clear.

8   If the fuel filter separating water from fuel has a glass bowl look for signs of water, debris and fine black, thread-like strands. These indicate biological growth in the tanked fuel which if left untreated blocks fuel lines and injectors. It is caused by not treating and filtering fuel before adding it to the tank. The cure is drain and clean the tank, fuel lines and injectors. When that is done then you replace the filters. Another negotiating point when discussing the price.

9   There should be a filter on the raw seawater side. What condition is it in?

10 Is the engine coolant clean, up to level and containing the correct amount of antifreeze?

11 Check that the engine mounts are in good condition and rust free.

12 Check the propshaft. Is the flexible coupling in good condition? Is there any indication that it has been placed under undue strain and is

beginning to fail? If there is no flexible coupling, find out what stops the gearbox being torn apart if a line fouls the prop. With flexible couplings it is almost impossible to tell if the propshaft is properly aligned, but one sign is undue engine vibration when running in gear.

13   Check the stern gland for signs of leaking.

14   Check the stern bearing by pushing the propeller from side to side. There should be no movement. If there is, it needs replacing. If there is a P-bracket, the shaft should not move when pushed from side to side. Check for damage where the P-bracket enters the hull. It has been known for boats to be lifted out of the water with a lifting sling round the P-bracket.

15   Check the engine controls.

16   Check that all the engine instrumentation works.

Engine compartment

Even for purists who regard engines as the work of the devil and propellers a clever form of egg whisk, engines are still the principal means of battery charging. Even purists may rely on electronics. It is important that when you need power the engine starts first time, every time. Older engines are

An engine mount can be seen in the bottom right-hand corner of this picture. It is covered in rust and showing signs of age. If engine mounts break up at sea then you have an engine swinging around on the end of the propshaft. Securing it would be nearly impossible and the potential for fatal damage very high. There are four engine mounts on this engine and replacing them on this, or any other engine, is hard, expensive work. Again, not a fatal flaw but a good negotiating point.

likely to have problems unless they have been meticulously maintained from day one.

A well-maintained engine should look clean and tidy. There should be no signs of oil leaking into the bilges or around gaskets, pipes and hoses.

If possible, start the engine. If ashore, stick a hosepipe up the raw water intake hull fitting and turn the tap on. Does the engine start easily? Run it for a while. Does it blow out smoke, particularly when you increase the power? This is not a good sign. Does water come out of the exhaust? This is a good sign. Put the engine in and out of gear. Check for vibration and unusual movement in the propshaft. If there is, then it is likely that the propshaft is out of alignment and is placing unnecessary strain on the flexible coupling and gearbox. It also means that the propeller is running inefficiently and using more fuel than it should. When you have finished these checks then look at the fuel filter again and see if anything nasty has been pulled through from the tank.

If it is a saildrive engine check the hull seals and ask their age. They may be due for renewal. Look for any signs of damage that suggest that the engine may have received a knock. This could have damaged the seals.

Engine-hour meters lie. It may not have been fitted for the life of the engine or it may have been reset. If it is claimed that the engine has been recently overhauled, then this should be supported by detailed receipts. Otherwise, be suspicious and if concerned about the condition of the engine have it surveyed by a marine engineer.

Electrics

A reliable source of electrical power is essential. For most boats this is a 12-volt battery system charged from the engine alternator, perhaps supplemented by solar panels or a wind generator.

Large amounts of electrical and electronic equipment are standard on boats of all sizes and create complicated wiring harnesses. All wiring should have the largest cross section possible to reduce voltage drop. Is the wiring neatly tied to bulkheads? Are individual wires labelled? Are different uses identified by wires of different colours? Is there an up-to-date wiring diagram? Examine electrical connections for signs of corrosion. If the panel is fused, check the correct value of fuses are being used. If the panel relies on circuit breakers then check they work.

The battery bank should be split into domestic and engine-start batteries with sufficient batteries for each task. Check the ampere hours on each battery. Domestic batteries should be low-discharge batteries. How is the switching between batteries done? Can the domestic battery be switched to boost the engine-start battery in an emergency? Batteries should be securely strapped down and located as close to the alternator as possible to reduce charging losses through voltage drop. Is there a battery-state meter or a voltmeter which does the same job?

If the boat is wired for mains shore power, is its wiring clearly identified and cannot be confused with the 12-volt circuit?

Seacocks and hull fittings

Every seacock and hull fitting is a potential leak. The water pressure from a one inch hole a couple of feet underwater will sink most boats. All skin fittings should be pulled down onto a sandwich of a large backing pad with a generous filling of sealant.

The skin fittings for all drains and water intakes should have their own seacock and the hoses to this should be held on by two stainless steel jubilee clips.

A suitably-sized wooden plug should be taped down close to every skin fitting so that it can be found by touch and rammed into the hole should the fitting break.

Check that all seacocks and hull fittings are accessible – not just to turn on or off but to service and replace. All hull fittings should be pulled down onto substantial pads.

Deck fittings

Use the results of your deck check to find where every deck fitting comes through. Leaking deck fittings are a pain. Look closely for the least sign of water penetration. This can involve much contortion and shining your torch into places that have not seen light since the hull and deck were

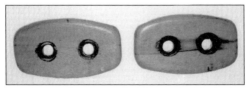

All deck fittings should be through-bolted onto backing pads. If they look like these then there is water coming in. These pads are made of a mahogany look-alike and the one on the right is beginning to break up. Any cracking in a backing pad means that it must be replaced.

brought together. Dark stains under the varnish of wooden bulkheads, or rust or discolouration around bolts, is a sign of water coming in. If this is not doing damage then at the very least it means that everything around them is soaked.

Leaking fittings need to be removed, cleaned up and refitted properly. At the worst, the fitting or its attachment may need to be redesigned. This can be another negotiating point when discussing the price.

Mast support

Check where a keel-stepped mast comes through the deck and how the fitting on the keel distributes its load. The rubber gaiter on a deck-stepped mast, which stops water coming below, tends to harden with time and will probably need replacing.

A deck-stepped mast can be in a tabernacle or a T- or U-channel. Check that these are on the centreline and that below deck the loads imposed by the mast are taken down the keel. This can be done by locating the tabernacle over a bulkhead or by a pole which acts as a continuation of the mast and runs down to the keel. This pole may be a wood or a steel rod or tube. Check how it is fixed to the tabernacle and the keel.

Finally

When your inspection schedule above and below decks is complete you will have several pages of notes, a good selection of photographs and a list of defects and deficiencies for each boat you examined. Now you have to decide which boats are worth a professional survey.

The loads from all deck-mounted masts must be carried down to the keel. Whatever does this job must be directly below the mast and fixed to the tabernacle, T- or U-channel and to the keel so that it cannot move about.

10 | Do I need a professional survey?

Having inspected each of your short-listed boats, and picked the best of the bunch, it is now time to consider if you need a professional survey to confirm your findings.

◆ WHY YOU NEED A SURVEY

Surveys are not cheap and not always necessary. You may be happy that your inspection has told you enough but there are times when you have no choice. Finance companies normally insist on a survey if you are using the boat as collateral on a loan or marine mortgage, and with older boats, your intended insurer may insist on a full structural survey before agreeing to provide cover.

Perhaps the owner has offered you a copy of a recent survey. This might make interesting reading. It may even support the findings from your inspection but if you are serious about buying and want reassurance that your money is being well spent, have your own survey carried out.

If you are buying a new, one-off boat or wish to check out a new production boat prior to accepting delivery, it might be useful to employ a marine surveyor to monitor the standard of workmanship. Boatyards and distributors are more likely to listen to a fellow professional telling them they have it wrong than to you. They may disagree, but when dealing with a fellow professional they know that they must support their disagreement with sound technical arguments.

◆ FINDING A SURVEYOR

The owner or broker conducting the sale may offer to find you a surveyor. This is tempting, especially if the boat is lying some distance from your home and you do not know any local surveyors, but there is an obvious clash of interests which is best avoided. However, it is only fair that surveyors charge mileage to cover their travelling expenses. So find one close to the boat, not to your home.

Check out your surveyor's area of expertise before employing them.

Surveyors normally specialise in particular types of boats. Being human, this does not prevent them earning a crust by agreeing to inspect boats outside their normal experience. There is nothing wrong with this practice but it is better to use a surveyor familiar with the type of vessel you plan to buy. It is also useful if they are yachtsmen with the practical insight that comes from sailing similar types of boat. For wooden hulls make sure that you find a surveyor familiar with wooden boat construction.

Yacht surveyors rarely carry out detailed engine surveys. If you are concerned about the condition of the boat's engine then it may be worthwhile having an engine survey carried out by a qualified marine engineer.

The websites of the various surveyors' associations list their members and their contact details. Some insurance companies and various other websites can also provide lists of surveyors. Some sites offer search facilities to find surveyors, not only by region or country, but by options like steel or GRP.

◆ SURVEYORS' ASSOCIATIONS

There is no legal requirement for a marine surveyor to join any professional association or hold a qualification in marine surveying. Traditionally, surveyors came from the ranks of naval architects, marine engineers, ship and boatbuilders and experienced seamen. The closest to a formal qualification in surveying for most surveyors is membership of a professional association such as the Yacht Brokers, Designers and Surveyors Association (YBDSA) in the UK. In the USA there are the International Institute of Marine Surveyors (IIMS), Society of Consulting Marine Engineers and Surveyors (SCMES), the National Association of Marine Surveyors Inc (NAMS) and the Society of Accredited Marine Surveyors Inc (SAMS). Membership of associations comes in various grades reflecting the expertise of the member.

Some professional associations endorse courses in marine surveying run by various training organisations. The first of these qualifications was the Diploma in Marine Surveying introduced by Lloyd's Maritime Academy in 1998. In the UK the YBDSA has approved a course in yacht and small craft surveying run by the International Boatbuilding Training College in Lowestoft.

The cost of a survey

The YBDSA does not have lists of recommended or even typical charges. When it comes to negotiating a price for the survey the advice is to ring round several suitable surveyors and take the one offering the best deal.

◆ EXCLUSION CLAUSES

When you receive a surveyor's report it may be so non-committal that you wonder why you bothered having a survey carried out. Statements are frequently qualified by phrases like *as far as could be ascertained/seen/ established*, or it *appeared/may be/is possible that*. To the uninitiated reader the boat may or may not be seaworthy and the only certainty apart from its name is that, as far as the surveyor can ascertain, it has not yet sunk. Surveyors have a highly developed aversion to firm opinions because this exposes them to charges of negligence. Under contract law, surveyors have a duty of care towards whoever employs them to make the survey. This is you, even if the survey has been arranged through a broker or some other third party. How far this duty of care extends depends on the terms of the contract you have with the surveyor.

Some surveyors restrict their survey to matters which can be assessed without destructive testing or physically dismantling parts of the boat. This is fair. Others limit their duty of care by inserting a clause in their standard contract excluding any liability for negligence. Some avoid answering any questions over their report by excluding *all* liability for *all* the advice which they may give and *all* the opinions they offer.

Surveys are often arranged by telephone or email and should you only become aware of exclusion clauses after you have agreed to the survey being carried out, then the surveyor would find it difficult to enforce any exclusions. This is cold comfort since you would probably need the support of the courts to win the day. So, if you are arranging a survey over the telephone ask about exclusions before agreeing and negotiate their exclusion.

Happily, regardless of any exclusions, courts assume that the surveyor will carry out the survey with the skill and expertise expected of any competent surveyor carrying out that type of survey.

◆ PROFESSIONAL INDEMNITY

If, as a result of a surveyor's mistake, you face a huge repair bill it seems only fair that the surveyor should bear the costs of putting matters right. Against this eventuality every prudent surveyor has personal indemnity insurance covering any errors or omissions they may make in the course of a survey. Membership of many professional associations make this insurance cover mandatory. Surveyors often do not mention this insurance because these policies frequently contain a clause saying that the existence of the policy should not be disclosed by the surveyor.

◆ BRIEFING A SURVEYOR

None of this detracts from the value of a good survey but it underlines the value of considering what you expect from a survey and the importance of instructing the surveyor accordingly.

Allowing a broker, or some other third party, to arrange the survey confuses the issue over who is instructing the surveyor. You are paying for the survey but it is possible for the surveyor to argue that he has been instructed by the broker who he believed was acting as your agent.

Arranging a survey through a third party, or accepting a surveyor's standard contract without question and then leaving them to decide what the survey involves, is not a sensible way of spending your money. It is not that the surveyor will do a poor job – few do – it is that he may not do the job you expect and want.

You must first decide whether you wish to have a condition survey or a condition and valuation survey. Banks, finance houses and insurance companies often ask that the surveyor puts a price on the boat and base their loan on what the surveyor thinks it is worth and not what you actually paid. This is called a valuation survey. Some surveyors charge extra for putting a price on a boat.

Otherwise, what you want is a condition survey and how far this goes depends in part on whether or not you are prepared to accept the costs of any destructive survey work. 'Destructive' is used loosely. It is not ripping the boat apart. It could be as simple as removing and inspecting some fastenings on a wooden boat or opening up to check an otherwise inaccessible area but the work involved and making it good afterwards carry a price that you must pay. Will the owner agree to this work being done and do you place a cash limit on it?

Your own inspection will have thrown up areas of concern where it is wise to have the reassurance of an expert opinion, especially when negotiating the price. Without mentioning specific faults, draw the surveyor's attention to these areas and instruct him to check and include the results in his report. You will probably agree the scope of the survey orally but confirm this in writing as soon as possible afterwards so that any misunderstanding can be resolved before the inspection is carried out.

◆ PREPARING THE BOAT

If the boat is afloat then it ought to be lifted out and power washed ready for the inspection. You pay for this unless you have persuaded the vendor to foot the bill or made an agreement to deduct the cost from the purchase price if you decide to buy it. Lifting out GRP yachts some days before the inspection, and allowing them to dry out, is good practice. Using a moisture meter on boats that have just been lifted out can lead to false readings from residual moisture in the paint layers or gel coat. Even salt residue on the hull can affect readings, underlining the importance of a thorough fresh-water power wash.

Make it clear to the yard that the boat must be out of the water and ready for the surveyor's arrival. If it is not then you may be billed by the surveyor for a wasted visit or for his time spent hanging around while the boat is lifted out.

◆ SUBJECT TO SURVEY

Before arranging the survey, a broker may expect you to go through the ritual of making an offer subject to survey and make a deposit of around 10 per cent of the asking price. If at all possible avoid this route. Take it and you have made a commitment to purchase this boat and backed it up with hard cash. You can only pull out of the deal if the survey reveals 'very serious' defects or the boat is found to be 'materially unsatisfactory'.

For lesser defects you are expected to negotiate a reduction in the asking price. Should the surveyor's report reveal failings that you consider so serious as to be unacceptable and if the broker disagrees with this then you will:

1   be locked into negotiations over the price;
2   head for the courts;
3   walk away leaving your deposit behind.

None of these is a satisfactory solution. If you do not make an offer 'subject to survey' then all you lose is the surveyor's fee.

◆ THE SURVEYOR'S REPORT

Once the surveyor has completed his work then he will probably give you an oral report covering the main points of his findings. Hear what he has to say but wait for the full written report before making any decision about purchasing.

Surveyors tend to use a standard form. The first point to check is whether or not the report covers all the points you raised. If there is no reference to any of the points you specifically instructed him to look at then ask for an explanation. The photographs you took in the course of your inspection may be helpful in ensuring that you are both talking about the same point and, if necessary, he can return to the boat and check the points you query at his own expense. Failing that, he is not paid and you use the money to commission another surveyor.

◆ USING THE SURVEYOR'S REPORT

Once you are happy with the report then read between its fuzzy lines and decide if you wish to proceed. Be realistic; you are not buying a new boat.

Defects are inevitable. The question is, can you live with them? From your own inspection and the surveyor's report you can prepare and cost out a list of the work needed to bring the boat up to standard. Classify each item on this list as:

1 *Fair wear and tear* These are the sort of flaws you would expect to find on a boat of this age and type. They mostly involve items like tired cushions, sails, engines and rigging reaching the end of their safe working life. These defects should not come as a surprise and are the type of flaws where there is a good argument that the cost of making good is shared between you and the seller. Fair's fair. You may not be buying a new boat but the seller should not expect his deferred maintenance to be paid for by the new owner.

2 *Serious but repairable faults* These are major defects like replacing leaking chain plates, damaged headsail foils, or upgrading stemhead fittings or tackling an attack of osmosis. These are costly items beyond normal annual maintenance and it is reasonable to expect the full cost of the remedial work to be reflected in the asking price.

3 *Serious but unrepairable defects* Given time and money, almost any defect can be repaired. For you, unrepairable means not that the price is too high but you would never be happy with a repair, however well it is carried out. This is when you make your excuses and leave.

Otherwise, either open negotiations over the price, and buy this boat, warts and all, or move to the next on your list and repeat this exercise until you have found a boat that meets your standards.

11 | Berthing arrangements

Berthing devours almost 40 per cent of your annual budget and is the area where you can save the most cash. It is easy to believe that if you wish to berth a boat, then it must be in a marina. This is partly because the growth in marinas saw many of the cheap berths and moorings that were tucked away in the remoter corners of harbours disappear and partly because we have grown accustomed to the shoreside facilities that marinas provide. It is estimated that there are around 450,000 to 500,000 boats in the UK and about 250 coastal marinas providing in the region of 50,000 berths. In other words, around 90 per cent of boats seem to be managing quite well without the expense of a marina berth. So, do not fall into the trap of believing that the only place you can park a boat is in a marina. There are cheaper options but you will need to consider:

- Type of boat
- Type of sailing
- Harbour dues
- Club membership fees
- Travelling costs
- Berthing costs

◆ TYPE OF BOAT

It is sensible to explore possible berthing arrangements before you buy your dream boat. What you learn can affect your choice of boat or where you decide to keep it. If you are buying a cruising yacht of 28–30ft (8–9m) your berthing options are narrowed to either a marina or permanent swinging mooring. But there are other types of boat that need special consideration:

Bilge keelers and centreboarders
If your boat can take the ground, then a drying mooring becomes a possibility. Drying moorings are at the cheaper end of the market because they are only accessible two or three hours either side of high water. Since the tides have a nasty habit of clashing with sailing timetables, this sometimes leaves you the choice of going to sea in the small dark hours or staying at

home. If you cannot accept this, then a drying mooring, however financially attractive, is not for you.

A variation on a drying mooring is a marina with a lock or sill holding back water and keeping the boats inside afloat at low water. Entering or leaving is still restricted to an hour or so either side of low water. Even so, the prices tend to be in line with those of any other marina.

Multihulls

Many marinas charge multihulls extra for their berth, sometimes as much as double their normal fee, which makes their usual scary price absolutely terrifying. On the plus side, multihulls are ideal for drying moorings or shallow-water swinging moorings.

Trailer sailers

Trailer sailers can be parked on the front drive but neighbours may object to having their view obscured by what seems to them to be a very large boat and there is the very real chance that a passing thief will hitch up your boat and tow it away, so you must invest in tow bar locks and wheel clamps for the trailer.

Some local authorities have rules about parking caravans in streets and driveways and may see no difference between a yacht on a trailer and a hut on wheels. If they do agree, then they may levy a parking charge. Check this out before committing yourself to keeping your boat at home.

If parking your boat on the front drive is impossible you may be able to keep it on its trailer (with the mast up) in the club or marina yard. This may be in a designated trailer park or any vacant corner but either option is cheaper than keeping it afloat. With luck there will be cheap, possibly even free, access to a ramp to launch your boat when you wish to sail.

If keeping your boat at home or in the club yard is out of the question then it may be possible to come to an arrangement with a local friendly farmer to keep your boat in his yard or in a corner of a fallow field.

You may find it worthwhile asking around at your local industrial estate. In the current economic climate, small factory owners may be interested in earning some extra cash by renting you some space on their hard standing. You may be lucky enough to find secure parking for your boat as an added bonus.

With trailer sailers there are launching fees to pay each time you sail and also the bother of stepping and unstepping the mast each time, which tends to rule out a quick evening sail.

Dinghies

Sailing dinghies can be taken home and kept on the front drive or even in the garage, though it is often more convenient to keep them in the club dinghy park. The charges for this are normally modest.

For dinghy and open boat sailors, parking your boat on its trailer in the yacht club yard is probably the cheapest and most convenient form of berthing.

◆ TYPE OF SAILING

Racing

If you race, then it is convenient to keep your boat close to those of your fellow competitors. This suggests a club mooring and certainly rules out berthing your boat some hours' sail away from the rest of the fleet or on a tide-restricted drying mooring.

Day and weekend sailing

Day and weekend sailors like to berth as close to the open sea as possible. This is a difficulty for a budget sailor as this type of berth is twice as expensive as one in a distant creek two or three hours' sail upriver. But although upriver moorings are cheaper, the time it takes to reach open water makes daysailing impossible and weekend cruises difficult.

Cruising

Those who make one or two long cruises a year are not over concerned about ready access to the open sea and do not mind beginning them with a downriver cruise provided it saves them money.

Live-aboards

Live-aboards are a special case. Sea gipsies tend to follow the sun, moving from one anchorage to another and when they arrive in an anchorage, they will spend days, sometimes weeks, before moving on. Their boats are fitted out so that they can live almost independently of shoreside facilities. For them, berthing charges are limited to paying occasional harbour dues.

Others choose to live aboard and keep their nine-to-five job. Their boat is more a floating apartment than a seagoing vessel and they need access to shoreside power and water and somewhere to park their car. This points them towards a marina and marinas take contrary views on live-aboards. Some look favourably on them. Out of self-interest, live-aboards keep a watchful eye over the marina and can be relied upon to report any repairs needed to the pontoons or their facilities. More important they will be quick to notice any unusual behaviour and are, in practice, an unpaid security force. In marinas which see live-aboards in this light there is the chance of negotiating favourable rates.

For their own reasons, other marinas discourage live-aboards by charging them higher rates (usually on the grounds that they make more use of the facilities) and placing restrictions on car parking and even the number of visitors they can receive and the times when these visitors may come.

If you intend to live aboard berthed in a marina then check this out before committing yourself to a particular marina.

◆ HARBOUR DUES

Some harbours have always charged leisure craft harbour dues in addition to berthing charges levied by marinas. More are following their example. Some clubs and marinas have negotiated a bulk discount. The saving is not huge but it is welcome.

◆ CLUB MEMBERSHIP FEES

Some yacht clubs have berths on piles or pontoons which they offer to members at below commercial rates. The first catch is that you must first be a member and the second that you may have to join a waiting list until a berth becomes available.

◆ TRAVELLING COSTS

There are regional and national differences in berthing charges. Berths in the remoter parts of the country are normally cheaper than those in sailing areas close to large towns and cities. It is possible to berth a large boat in a distant marina or anchorage for the price of a boat half the size close to home but if you travel enormous distances to reach your boat then the savings quickly disappear in travel costs.

It is tempting to equate the price of travel to the cost of fuel but as any motoring organisation is happy to explain, fuel is only part of your running costs. If you take account of the wear and tear on the car, meals eaten en route and any ferry charges or road tolls then a rough guide to the real travel costs is twice what you spend on fuel.

Foreign berths

In some European countries, berths are cheap compared to the UK and the availability of cheap flights has brought them within economic reach. For some, keeping their boat abroad is no more costly than parking it in a UK marina but with the advantages of sunshine and exotic cruising grounds. Distant berths, whether at home or abroad, are, by their very nature, not conducive to day or weekend sailing.

◆ BERTHS

Berths come in five varieties: marinas, piles, trots, swinging moorings and drying berths.

Marinas

Marinas first appeared in the United States during the 1930s and reached the UK just in time to provide the extra berths needed for the ever-increasing number of plastic boats that began appearing in the 1960s. Marinas are expensive but for your money you get ease of access to your boat, good security and a wide range of facilities, not all of which are free. Water is standard but power normally comes at a price. In some marinas you can also plug into cable TV and the internet. Marinas also have easy access to shoreside shops, cafes and restaurants.

Marina charges Market forces rule: the more popular a sailing area, the higher its marina charges. In England, prices are highest along the south coast but even here there are variations. As befits its claim to be the home of yachting, the Solent area probably has the highest berthing charges.

Town centre marinas are often several hours sail upriver, far from any cruising or racing grounds. Consequently their charges tend to be less than marinas which have direct access to the sea. If you can accept that each sail begins and ends with a couple of hours chugging up or down a busy waterway, they may be a worthwhile option.

All marina charges are per foot or metre based on LOA, as measured from the very tip of the bow, including anchors on bow rollers, bowsprits and the pulpit overhang to the far end of transom hung rudders; it also includes rudders, outboard motors and anything else sticking out at the stern. Fractions of a metre are often rounded up. Your 10-metre boat can suddenly acquire an extra metre. Additional charges for multihulls are common.

All marinas try to park as many boats as they can in the smallest space available. Often the most demanding manoeuvres you make are entering and leaving your berth. It is no surprise marinas insist on every boat carrying several million pounds' worth of third party insurance.

Pricing schemes are complicated with different rates for day, week, month, summer or winter season or shoreside storage besides an annual rate. Discounts may be offered to members of local yacht clubs and there may be special deals on offer. These are not always advertised so ask before agreeing a deal. Berths are normally paid for in advance. For an additional charge, marinas may allow berth holders to pay their annual berth rental in monthly instalments.

Lifting in or out For an additional fee most marinas lift out boats either for a refit or for winter storage ashore which is occasionally cheaper than lying alongside. Restricted yard space sometimes limits the time each boat is allowed ashore to a few days, and long-term winter storage ashore is not possible. If there are limits on time ashore then there may also be penalties if you exceed them.

Marinas in or near town centres are often heavily developed with shops, offices and flats and have no yard space at all. If you need to lift out, then you go elsewhere. If this is for less than a month then marina price structures usually see you paying for yard space wherever you choose to lift out, while still paying for a berth at the marina.

MARINA CHARGES

Marina pricing structures are so varied and complex, that direct comparisons between marinas, and deciding upon the best deal, is extremely difficult. The annual berthing fee is often just a starting point for additional charges that can add 20–25 per cent to your bill. As always, the devil is in the small print. Marina pricing strategies include:

1   Rounding LOA to the nearest metre, 9.6m becomes 10.0m. This adds around 4.2 per cent to your annual fee.

2   Rounding LOA up in metre jumps, 9.01m becomes 10.0m, which adds about 9 per cent to your annual fee.

3   Pricing bands: 7–10m is hard on 7m boats and especially those rounded up from 6.01m.

4   A minimum starting LOA, say 10 or 12m, which all boats under 10m (or 12m) pay regardless.

5   Offers of six months afloat and six months ashore with each period priced separately with lift out and in added on.

6   Charging for car parking.

7   Some include electricity in the berthing fee, some charge at cost and some sell power at a mark-up.

8   Live-aboards are charged extra or not allowed.

9   Haul-out and power wash are sometimes priced separately. This normally adds 10–15 per cent to your berthing fee.

10 Some lift out fees include blocking up; some do not; sometimes cradle hire is extra.

11 Taking down and putting up masts on sailing yachts is charged separately. Mast storage is often an extra.

12 Many marinas offer the option of paying by instalments, usually either in 3 or 10 instalments which raises the price by 2 to 10 per cent respectively. A few will offer a reduction on up-front payment.

13 Frequently, winter storage ashore is charged in addition to the annual berth fee. Variations include three or four weeks free or placing a maximum on time out of water.

14 There are often restrictions on the work that owners are allowed to carry out to their own boats before approved contractors, who usually pay the marina a fee for being an approved contractor, must be used.

15 Ask what their prices were over the last two or three years to have some idea of how their prices will change. Most price increases are above the rate of inflation. In 2009 when the UK was approaching negative inflation figures, some marinas were raising prices 3–6 per cent.

MARINA CHARGES IN THE USA

Annual berthing charges in the USA are normally based on a monthly rate per foot of LOA. Occasionally rates are banded into, for example, boats under 30ft and boats over 30ft and then there is a long list of extra services which may, or may not, be built into the headline figure. These can include:

- LOA may be boat length or slip length, whichever is the greater.
- Power
- Water
- Pump out
- Trash
- Phone jack

- Cable TV
- Wireless Internet
- Taxes
- Department of Natural Resources fees

So, before comparing prices discover how much is added to the base fee to discover the all-up moorage charge.

Like everywhere there are up and down market marinas with prices to match. Typically they start at just under $2,500 to nearly $9,000 a year with an average of around $4,000.

Piles

A pile mooring involves picking up a line running between two posts and mooring fore-and-aft between the posts. In tidal waters the line is normally on a buoyed ring around the pile to allow for rise and fall with the tide. Access is by dinghy which you leave on your mooring when out for the day.

Piles are normally found only in sheltered waters but seen from the viewpoint of a small, overloaded dinghy, shelter offered by a pile berth is relative.

Lack of ready access is an excellent security measure but leaving attractive items like liferafts, MOB systems and anchors on view when you are not aboard is unwise.

Pile moorings are being phased out by many harbour authorities nowadays.

Trots

A trot is a pile mooring where the posts are replaced by buoys. Just like a pile mooring, you pick up a floating line and use it to moor fore-and-aft between the buoys. As the buoys rise and fall with the tide, boats can move around more on the trot mooring than a pile mooring.

Swinging mooring

A swinging mooring is where boats moor to a single buoy and how they lie is determined by the wind and the tide. They tend to be further from shore and are more exposed to wind and seas than piles or trots. In some conditions, reaching and boarding your boat can amount to a cruise in its own right.

Some trots are made up of parallel lines of boats. This multiplies the chances of hitting another boat and makes going on and coming off your mooring more demanding than a single line of boats.

Swinging moorings are always remote and peace of mind requires excellent ground tackle. In hilly countryside, katabatic squalls have been known to carry boats and their ground tackle out to sea.

Drying berths

A drying berth is a fore-and-aft mooring that dries at low tide. They are best for multihulls or bilge or lifting-keel yachts that can safely take the ground. In soft mud, long-keeled yachts may sit upright using legs, but this is not a good idea as a long-term solution, particularly if the bottom is uneven, for as the tide falls one leg may sink further into the mud than the other, causing the boat to heel. Over successive tides this heel can increase to a point where the boat is lying on its side.

Drying berths are only accessible when there is enough water to reach them by dinghy and are found in:

- Small drying harbours
- Drying areas of large harbours/ports
- Remote creeks and inlets.

There may be a secure dinghy park where you can leave your dinghy between cruises. If not, you may have to take it home between sails, and long-term car parking may be a problem.

◆ FINDING A BERTH

In the more popular sailing areas, your chosen marina may be full and have a waiting list. Otherwise, finding a marina berth is just a matter of negotiating the best price and handing over the money.

Marinas tend to squeeze out berths tucked away in odd corners and dead ends of harbours but these secluded and cheap berths are still there if you take the trouble to look.

The budget option

Berths on piles, trots, swinging moorings and mud berths are normally let by the year and tend to be run by harbour authorities, local councils, yacht clubs or, occasionally, individuals. Finding one usually requires some detective work that begins by exploring the remoter creeks and corners of harbours and rivers. You are looking for small clusters of yachts where you least expect to see them. Having found them, the next task is to find out who administers these berths, what they cost and how you can be allocated a berth.

Their cheapness makes them popular and there is often a waiting list. Get your name on any waiting list as early as possible. When you do get a mooring, do not give it up to save some money while you haul out for the winter, for in the spring you may find yourself at the back of the queue for moorings. This means that you may be adding the cost of a winter berth ashore to that of your mooring. Berth holders often come together to form an association or club to look after their interests and have either communal arrangements for winter berths or will advise where to find the best deal.

These berths are charged per mooring not boat size. Work afloat is limited to tasks which can be carried out using hand- or battery-powered tools. Using heaters or dehumidifiers are out of the question. Loading up for a cruise is best done at an alongside berth for which there may be a charge.

◆ COMPARING BERTHING COSTS

As a rough and ready rule of thumb, a pile, trot or swinging mooring is about 15–30 per cent the cost of a marina berth. Berth for berth, yacht club berths tend to be the cheapest of all and some clubs have pontoon berths with facilities rivalling any marina. Waiting lists for club berths are inevitable and every club has its Byzantine points system to allocate berths without fear or favour. Length of membership rates highly and if you are serious about buying a boat and want a club berth then joining a suitable club and putting your name on the waiting list for berths as early as possible is a wise move.

12 | Personal equipment

Like all sports, yachting has its own iconic brands of clothing and equipment and it is tempting to want to go to a chandlery and choose the best new gear. However, this is not an option for the budget sailor who will be looking for cheap bargains.

◆ SAFETY EQUIPMENT

Penny pinching does not apply to personal safety equipment such as lifejackets, harnesses and tethers. Safety gear must be of the highest quality; it must be able to do its job with a wide margin to spare and tough enough to survive the abuse that comes with life aboard a small boat. You may never need any of this equipment, but if you do then its job is to keep you and your crew alive to sail another day. At such times it is a bargain, whatever it costs. Consider investing in professional-quality equipment. Incredibly, safety lights, crotch straps and sprayhoods are extras on some leisure lifejackets.

There should be an exposure suit for everyone aboard. One-use suits are cheap but they appear to be made from the same material as polythene

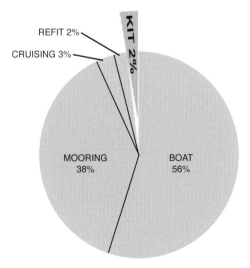

Personal equipment costs are among the lesser elements that make up the overall budget.

shopping bags and probably last as long. This is possibly doing them a disservice, but liferafts are a harsh environment and investing in a better-made, stronger exposure suit may give you the edge you need to survive. It is amazing how quickly water pours through the smallest rip in an exposure suit, rendering it useless.

◆ KEEPING WARM

Keeping warm depends on keeping out the wind and putting as many layers of air as possible between you and the outside world when you venture into the cockpit or on deck. As the temperature rises, you can take layers off and as it falls they go back on.

Layers come in three types and each does a particular job. There is a base layer to wick away perspiration and keep your skin dry. Next comes the mid-layer which is intended to keep you warm, and finally there is the top layer which aims to keep out the wind and wet.

You can wear top branded clothing from the skin outwards but there is no evidence that lesser-known, cheaper brands perform any less well for a fraction of the price. Many shops, not just sailing outlets, sell thermal clothing. A top-of-the-range windproof fleece can cost ten times that of a lesser-known brand. A woollen jersey or bobble hat does the same job whatever its logo.

Most sailing shoes claim to have soles that stick to waterfalls. In the real world the deck, not your shoes, should be non-slip so that you are safe whatever your footwear. The only requirement for a pair of deck shoes is that they are comfortable and do not mark, scuff or chip the deck.

◆ KEEPING DRY

It is obvious that waterproofs should keep you dry. But how dry? Complete dryness means stopping rain and spray coming in and letting perspiration out. Materials for keeping water out have been around for decades but we had to wait until the 1980s before breathable fabrics arrived which let perspiration out.

This was a godsend to anyone involved in vigorous physical activity. For the first time, keeping out rain and spray did not mean living in a sweaty dampness that chilled you the instant you stopped jumping around.

As always, there is a catch. Just like the cheapest non-breathable oilies, a set of top quality breathable waterproof jacket and trousers will still leak, creating a slowly growing damp spot that spreads from your neck, around your chest, across your back and then downwards to your toes, because seals, if fitted, are never perfect and stretch, crack and curl as they age, allowing water in. Seawater does *not* behave like perspiration and disappear through the breathable membrane, leaving you warm and dry.

If you go overboard wearing separate oilskin jacket and trousers you are soaked to the skin within seconds of hitting the water. Good seals slow down the exchange of water warmed by your body heat with cold sea water but the heat loss is relentless. If it is important that you stay dry or if there is a real risk of falling into the water (open boats and dinghy sailors are at particular risk, then the answer is a breathable dry suit with proper water-proof seals. It costs about a third of the price of top brand water proofs and keeps you warm much longer if you unexpectedly find yourself in the water.

◆ HOW OFTEN DO YOU NEED WATERPROOFS?

Adverts for waterproofs claim that they offer 'day long comfort' or contain statements saying that anyone offshore sailing needs 'full storm protection, because they are 'on deck for extended periods of time'. But it has been estimated that about a third of all boats never or rarely leave their berths. This does not prevent their owners stepping aboard dressed to survive the ultimate storm. The rest of us tend to go to sea in good weather during the summer months. The number of occasions we encounter weather so bad that it justifies kitting up probably does not reach double figures each year, and then each occasion lasts for no more than a few hours. Waterproofs are worn mostly as windbreakers or as maritime Macintoshes in rain showers, not to ward off seas breaking over the boat.

Think hard and realistically about what you expect from your oilskins and do not buy anything above those requirements.

◆ SOURCING PERSONAL AND OTHER EQUIPMENT

Finding the right equipment means:

1   Specifying what you expect an item of equipment to do
2   How well you expect it to perform.

So look for kit that meets your standards. Buying the best kit for the job is not the same as buying the most expensive and the best source may not be a yacht chandlery.

Yacht chandlers

Most yachting chandlers offer a range of different-quality waterproofs which can be classed as: best, medium and budget quality or, stressing its nautical connections: ocean, offshore and inshore. The best costs twice or three times more than budget quality. Often the most obvious differences are the logos and lettering but the price variations can also reflect differences in specification, materials and methods of manufacture. Whether the extra expenditure between best and budget is justified is a personal decision but rain and spray are equally wet wherever you are and some of the nastiest breaking seas you are ever likely to encounter are found in inshore waters. So, if it is good enough for inshore why not wear it offshore?

Commercial chandlers

Fishermen want durable, practical foul weather gear. Their lives and livelihood depends upon their foul weather gear keeping them warm and dry, summer and winter. It must also withstand use and abuse far beyond that found on a yacht. It may not look fashionable but it will do the job and be much less expensive.

Mountaineering suppliers

Mountaineering equipment stores are worth checking out. Climbers take their foul weather gear into sub-zero blizzards and subject it to the most fearsome wear and tear. Yet top-quality mountaineering waterproofs cost about half that of sailing gear.

Motorcycle shops

For motorcyclists, a gentle shower turns into the driving spray we expect from a full-blown storm and they stay dry hour after hour. Modern bikers' leathers are heavy-duty breathable fabrics that are abrasion resistant to a degree unimaginable in yachting oilskins for they must protect the wearer from road burn should they lose their wheels and slide along the road. Bikers' gear looks out of place on a yacht but, like mountaineering gear, it costs about half the price of top-range yachting gear. Does usage and style alone explain the price difference?

Construction workers' catalogues

Health and Safety rules lay down that workmen exposed to the elements wear suitable protective clothing, not just against the hazards of their work but against the weather. Thumb through the catalogue from any supplier of protective clothing to the construction trade and be surprised. Foul weather gear starts with base layers and travels outwards through shirts, pants and fleeces (normal and windproof), to breathable trousers and jackets. It is sophisticated, smart, hardwearing and cheap. Workmen like high-visibility clothing and though their waterproofs may have few logos they are liberally striped with the retro-reflective material that most sailing gear restricts to hoods and, perhaps, cuffs.

◆ ADDING UP THE SAVINGS

You have to decide whether the price of top-quality clothing reflects a proportionate increase in durability and performance over cheaper gear or if you are just buying a logo.

Realistically, most of us settle for buying reasonable quality, durable personal gear which probably costs between a third to a half the price of top-range yachting equipment with no significant difference in performance. Hunt around and you may save as much as 60 per cent of the cost.

Personal equipment	Top of range price	Mid-range price	Budget price
Hat	£30.00	£20.00	£5.00
Base layer	£45.00	£35.00	£5.00
Layer 2	£130.00	£100.00	£18.00
Fleece	£110.00	£80.00	£10.00
Oilskin jacket	£489.00	£290.00	£20.00
Oilskin trousers	£190.00	£130.00	£10.00
Sea boots	£190.00	£65.00	£15.00
Deck shoes	£140.00	£50.00	£20.00
Gloves	£35.00	£25.00	£5.00

A cruise is when you leave your home port for one night or more; otherwise you are daysailing. Berthing away from your home port involves finding somewhere to stay each night.

◆ MOTOR SAILING

Racing boats do most of their travelling under sail but a cruising yacht sailing from one port to another has a destination, not an ETA. If you have plenty of time you can arrive when winds and tides decree but there are occasions when waiting for the wind to serve is not an option. Drifting around in shipping lanes is one example and if you must be back in time for work on Monday morning, then light or contrary winds can make a mockery of any timetable. The temptation to switch on the engine becomes irresistible. At today's fuel prices this can be an expensive decision.

Reducing fuel consumption

Firstly, try to reduce fuel consumption by winning some progress from the sails. Getting a knot of wind is less work for the engine and this saves fuel. If you find yourself with light winds and a lumpy swell that leaves the sails banging and flapping, it might be necessary to put them away to avoid unnecessary wear. Otherwise any power you gain from the wind comes free. If the wind direction does not suit then consider beating with the engine running. This allows you to point higher than with the sails alone and make better time.

Secondly, always keep the engine revolutions as low as possible whilst maintaining an acceptable rate of advance. As you approach your maximum hull speed, pull the throttle back a little. Pushing your boat up its own bow wave is wasting fuel. How many revolutions you need to reach hull speed varies with sea conditions. In a calm sea it is surprising how few are needed to maintain a decent cruising speed. In a steep, short sea that tries to stop the boat every other wave, you might need twice as much power to make any progress at all.

Thirdly, when you are motor sailing, from time to time pull the engine into neutral and check progress under sail alone. It is easy to become so accustomed to the sound of the engine chugging away that you fail to notice that the wind has perked up just enough to make motor sailing unnecessary.

Fine tuning

As part of your annual maintenance, clean and polish the propeller and make sure it is free from nicks and bends. It is surprising how little it takes to start a propeller cavitating and for its efficiency to start dropping away. A drop in efficiency of 5–10 per cent does not sound much but it is reflected in greater fuel consumption.

◆ BERTHING

Racing

When racers are away from home they normally go en masse and frequently by road. How else could a boat take part in Kiel, Cowes and Cork weeks and still have time to race every weekend? If they go by sea it is normally as part of a race or to a regatta with a neighbouring club, and reduced berthing fees have been negotiated on a tit-for-tat basis when the visit is returned. For racers, overnight fees in strange harbours are a small part of the annual sailing budget.

Cruising

Visiting new harbours and anchorages is at the very heart of cruising but overnight charges are now so high that the fees for a two-week cruise in UK waters could pay for a fortnight in the sun, including spending money. Add on to this the cost for a handful of weekends away each season and the total paid out in visitors' fees can approach a third to a half what you pay for your annual berth.

Unless you stay at home and settle for day sailing there are only two ways of cutting overnight berthing charges. First, arrange a cruise in company with several other yachts. These may be other club members or owners of the same class of boat. Agree an itinerary and then negotiate a block booking at the marinas where you plan to stay. This can produce substantial savings but it will not work in the more popular yachting areas.

The second method is to reduce the time spent in marinas to an absolute minimum. This is more for individuals rather than boats sailing in company; at one time this involved nothing more than steering clear of the most popular marina breeding grounds, but as marinas reach out to ever more remote locations this is becoming increasingly difficult.

It is, however, still possible to find budget berths. When you have decided on your cruising area, check out its harbours. Almanacs and pilots normally give berthing charges. If not, most harbours have a website advertising their charges and attractions.

MARINA OVERNIGHT BERTHING CHARGES (2009) (Based on 10m LOA)			
	Average	Max	Min
South-east Scotland	£18.42	£28.50	£9.75
North-west Scotland	£18.86	£26.40	£9.00
South Wales/Bristol Channel	£19.88	£31.20	£10.50
South-west Scotland	£20.71	£29.16	£13.50
Eastern England	£20.83	£38.70	£12.00
Northern Ireland	£23.37	£31.20	£16.80
South-east England	£23.46	£30.00	£12.00
North-east England	£23.73	£30.00	£7.50
South-west England	£24.23	£36.00	£6.48
North-west England	£25.40	£37.08	£18.00
Central south England	£29.93	£38.40	£12.00
UK average	£22.62		

Anchorages

Look in yachting pilot books. These often include anchorages which do not reach the almanacs. However, so many boats settle for cruising from marina to marina that even cruising pilots tend to include only the better known and more popular anchorages; sometimes the local harbour authority finds it worthwhile to send a boat round to collect anchoring fees.

The smaller, less frequented anchorages are still there. Finding them and learning their limitations just takes a little more work. If you study large-scale charts you will notice small bays and inlets where you could spend a night or two. Read up on the history of the coast. In the 18th and

19th centuries, small coasters used anchorages and harbours that, once the trade they served stopped, became forgotten.

Slowly you will build up a list of harbours and anchorages that are worth a visit without breaking the bank. It is usually worth the effort. There is something magical waking up in a small bay to greet the day and share the moment with nothing but a still sea, a sleeping landscape and a hot cup of coffee. Civilisation may be just over the hill but for an instant it is on another planet.

◆ ANCHORING

Anchoring is rapidly becoming a lost art. Many modern yachts make do with small bow fairleads instead of a decent bow roller. A lightweight anchor is fine for a lunch stop on a calm day but as you swing to tide and wind in the small hours of the night, any anchor can unhook and smaller anchors are more likely to forget to dig in again and let you go walkabout. Overnight anchoring requires substantial ground tackle that allows you to sleep safely. A good anchor and anchor rode are not cheap but they soon pay for themselves.

Anchoring when the weather is fine it is great fun but in poor weather a cockpit tent (or a very large boat) is almost essential for civilised life.

You also need an anchor light, bright enough to be seen but not so powerful it drains the battery. If there are shore lights visible, consider supplementing a fixed anchor light with a small flashing light so that other yachts entering the anchorage can pick you out against the shore lights.

Many anchorages are far from the beaten track. A dinghy is essential to go ashore and sometimes there is no handy jetty. An inflatable is light enough to drag easily above the high water mark but it does not take kindly to abuse and is the very devil to row. A small outboard engine is useful, almost essential. Rigid dinghies are better able to withstand the hard wear and tear of beaching and are easier to row or tow but they are heavier and occupy more deck space.

Sadly, if the anchorage is close to civilisation you may return from the hostelry to find your dinghy missing. If you leave it on a line astern overnight there is no guarantee it will be there in the morning. This means using wire strops as mooring lines and padlocks as knots. Consider distressing the paintwork to make the outboard look old and less appealing. Even then lock it to the transom. Drill holes in the oars and padlock them to the boat.

◆ GOING FOREIGN

If your timescale allows, UK based boats should consider going foreign. For some reason most marinas in mainland Europe charge about a third to a half the price of those in Britain. It is possible to take the standing mast route through Holland from Flushing in the south to Delfzijl in the north and spend most nights in free, canal-side berths. In practical terms this means that two to three weeks European cruising costs about the same or less than one week in UK waters.

A shoestring cruise requires more planning and preparation than simply heading for one of the more popular cruising grounds. It is hard work but in return it takes you away from overpriced marinas, and the frenetic overcrowded waters they serve, into less frequented, sometimes empty, quieter waters where the spirit of cruising lives on.

14 | The annual refit

It is a fundamental truth that the bigger a boat then the more it costs to maintain. There are no exceptions. If you wish to save money on the annual refit then the surest way is to buy a smaller boat.

There are five elements to your annual refit budget which offer some scope for savings:

- Hauling-out to work on your boat (and hauling-in)
- Planned maintenance
- Routine maintenance
- Consumables
- Learning the skills to do the work yourself

◆ HAULING-OUT

Where to haul-out

Think carefully about where to haul-out. Marinas lift boats out on demand, at a time to suit you, but may insist on adding a non-optional power wash and cradle hire to the bill. When you are ready to return your boat to the water, they lose no time in asking for more money. Unstepping, storing and stepping the mast is often another extra. Most marinas offer a variety of package deals on hauling-out which start with lifting out, sitting in the slings for an hour or so and then being put back in the water, through to lifting out and spending the winter in the yard. Always ask about these offers and whether or not one can be tailored to more closely match your needs and pocket.

Some yacht clubs have similar haul-out facilities to marinas and make them available to non-members, albeit at a higher rate than that for club boats. If you keep your boat in a marina, arranging to haul-out for a few days at the local yacht club can cut the cost of hauling-out and in by half or more.

Clubs with shoreside storage but no dedicated haul-out facilities often hire a crane and organise a mass lift-in and lift-out at the beginning and end of each season. The cost of the crane hire is shared amongst those having their boats lifted out. This is probably the cheapest of all haul-out options.

A club lift-out, which shares the costs amongst the boats involved, is the cheapest way of coming ashore for the winter. In clubs which are able to arrange this, you will probably find the skills that will help you with the work on your boat.

Yard facilities

Working ashore requires access to electrical power and water. A water supply can usually be arranged even if it means linking two or three hoses together.

If the yard has no electricity supply or has high charges for plugging into its supply then it is surprising how quickly a small generator pays for itself. Buy one which produces at least 1000 watts. This will provide enough power for most hand tools.

A power washer is great for cleaning hulls and decks. If you have access to power and water you can buy your own power washer for about the same price as a marina charges for washing down your yacht's hull when they lift the boat out. After the first year, power washing is free.

◆ MAINTENANCE

Routine maintenance

Routine maintenance is carried out between autumn and spring when most boats are out of the water. This is often called the annual refit which somehow implies that there is much work to be done, most of it requiring special nautical (and technical) skills. Some marinas and yards limit the work they allow owners to do to their own boats to a little gentlemanly painting and varnishing. Any other work must either be done by marina yard staff or their approved contractors. This makes the 'refit' very expensive. This is especially true of yards surrounded by apartments whose occupants may be disturbed by the noise from power tools. Marinas in this situation often place restrictions on days and time of day when you may work on your boat. Cut costs by avoiding marinas or yards which impose this type of limitation.

If you have bought a second-hand boat then the first one or two annual refits are spent making good any defects and deficiencies spotted during your pre-purchase inspection. The cost of this ought to be covered

Boat maintenance requires a wide range of practical, hands-on skills. In some clubs there are members who trade skills on a co-operative basis. These are good clubs to join. Be aware that some work, such as fitting LPG appliances, needs to be carried out by suitably qualified engineers.

by your cannily negotiated purchase price. Otherwise routine maintenance usually does not go much beyond:

- Cleaning and polishing the hull and making good any small blemishes that may have appeared during the course of the sailing season
- Antifouling below the waterline
- Renewing the boot topping
- Varnishing brightwork (woodwork)
- Winterising and commissioning the engine
- Changing fuel and oil filters and, just before putting the boat back in the water, commissioning the engine
- Valeting sails and checking the running and standing rigging

Most of this work requires nothing more than plain, time-consuming graft which demands no skill beyond a willingness to get your hands dirty: scraping off old antifouling, applying new, preparing and varnishing brightwork, cleaning and polishing the topsides and stripping and servicing gear such as winches. The cost of consumables such as filters, paints and sandpapers is almost nothing compared to the wallet-punishing hourly labour charges any yard worth its salt rightly demands for doing this work.

How much time an annual refit takes depends on your boat. GRP hulls are the least demanding and most forgiving to maintain. Next come steel hulls but only if they have been shot-blasted and painted using the right primers, under- and topcoats. Done correctly, the hull will need little attention for the next ten years or so. If you rely on household paints, the money you save on marine paint is paid for with a never ending (and losing) battle against rust.

Wooden hulls are the most demanding, and costly to refit. If you skimp they will rot before your eyes. The hull needs taking back to bare wood and repainted every couple of years. All brightwork must be meticulously maintained to keep water out. Any damage to paint or brightwork during the season must be made good immediately to prevent water reaching the wood.

Each refit begins by searching for any areas of rot that may have appeared during the season, cutting them out and making good. This requires a high level of woodworking skills and if you lack them you may have to take your boat to one of the few remaining yards with these skills.

◆ BUYING BUDGET CONSUMABLES AND EQUIPMENT

Money can be saved by buying compatible rather than branded fittings and consumables. Filters and fan belts bought through an approved dealer bearing the engine manufacturer's logo cost up to four times the price of generic filters and belts carrying a lesser-known name. They last just as long and can be only 25 per cent of the price of branded parts. This principle also holds good during major refits for items like engine mounts, alternators and flexible couplings.

Suppliers of filters and fan belts are found by going to *Yellow Pages* and looking under motor factors. Take an example of your current filter or fan belt with you and explain what you require. You are speaking to experts and if they cannot supply what you need then they will know some firm locally that can.

To say that engine mounts are nothing more than anti-vibration mountings may be stating the obvious but anti-vibration mountings are also used to fix machinery to factory floors, and it is possible that when you come to replace yours, much cheaper compatible mountings may be available. Check *Yellow Pages* for suppliers under engineering supplies.

Your car mechanic can probably point you towards a firm that can supply you with a compatible alternator for the boat's engine or a firm that can service the starter motor if it is playing up.

Galley equipment, pots, pans, plastic crockery and glasses and 12-volt domestic lights are remarkably similar to those found in caravan stores, where they are usually far cheaper than similar items in marine stores.

If you are considering fitting a warm-air heating system check out prices on those fitted to caravans and commercial vehicles.

If you need stainless steel screws, nuts, bolts, washers and other fixings, buy from a firm that specialises in supplying fixing products (*Yellow Pages* again!) to the construction trade. Their prices are less than a tenth of those at the local marine store.

Buy the brands of paints, oils and lubricants used by commercial vessels. If you are unsure what brands to ask for, talk to:

1 Your local fishing skippers
2 The commercial chandlers who supply them
3 The technical departments of paint manufacturers such as International, Leigh or Jotun

Their choice of topcoat or antifouling may not have the sheen desired by racing skippers but it will be more durable and economical and probably indistinguishable at ten paces. Further savings can be made by clubbing together with like-minded friends and buying paints and varnishes in bulk.

When new models of equipment appear on the market, chandlers often offer a discount on the old models they have in stock. Provided the new model has not rendered its predecessor obsolete this can be a route to substantial savings. If you must have the latest model you can try the old chestnut of ringing round suppliers for costs and then see if anyone will undercut the lowest price.

Where to buy cheaply

Boat jumbles can be a fruitful source of savings on second-hand equipment where haggling over the price is part of the fun but remember there is probably no redress if the equipment is faulty or does not perform as expected. Impulse buys, always a danger at boat jumbles, do not represent a saving if they are unnecessary or superfluous to requirements.

Buying from a known retailer over the internet is normally no different from buying over the counter or by mail order. With retailers that are new to you, ask around and find out how others rate them. A glossy website may not reflect the real scale of their business.

Internet shopping is, however, a good way of finding the best price for any item of equipment and if postage, packing, taxes and custom duties make the final cost unattractive then drawing your local supplier's attention to the base price may result in them offering a discount.

Bidding on eBay for second-hand goods is pretty much the same as shopping at boat jumbles except that you cannot see the goods before you buy and you have only one chance to haggle. eBay is also an outlet for suppliers who hold stocks of goods and sell on demand for a fixed price which is often well below that of your local shops even after post and packaging is added on.

If buying from abroad then above a certain value (it varies from country to country) it is normal to pay import duties and taxes. These are usually collected by the delivery firm on behalf of the customs authority and must be handed over before delivery is made. It is worth checking out how much these payments will amount to before buying for they can turn what seems to be a bargain into an expensive misjudgement.

◆ MAJOR REFIT

Every item of equipment has its useful working life. Regardless of how carefully fittings and equipment are maintained, there comes a time when the cost of keeping it in a safe working condition is close to the price of renewing it. It is time for a major refit.

A major refit is not taking the boat apart and rebuilding it. All fittings and equipment wear out at different rates. On a yacht a major refit usually deals with a single item such as replacing the standing rigging, the engine mounts or stern gland. Done properly, then apart from routine maintenance, you should not need to look at that item again for some years.

Rigging and sails

After about ten years your insurance company will probably insist on the standing rigging, including bottlescrews, being replaced. Somewhere in this period you would probably wish to renew the running rigging and the harder-worked sails.

If the mast is unstepped, remove the standing rigging and seek quotes from local rigging firms for its replacement. Check out commercial as well as marine rigging firms. You will find it far cheaper to buy the bottlescrews direct from the manufacturer or on the internet or eBay rather than from the rigging firm. Enter your requirements in the search engine and a long list of suppliers appears. On eBay it is not always necessary to bid for what you want. Many items are available on a 'buy it now' basis.

Some sail lofts take old sails in part exchange and refurbish them before putting them up for sale. Provided you can find a sail on their list which matches the dimensions of a sail you wish to replace, trading in your old sail for a refurbished sail is much cheaper than buying new.

Painting the hull

Painting the hull is done either because the original finish has lost its lustre and is looking shabby or you wish to upgrade the existing hull finish to protect your investment. Giving a GRP hull an epoxy topcoat dramatically reduces the risk of osmosis. Taking a steel hull back to bare metal and repainting can add years to its life. Wooden boats need repainting at regular intervals as part of their planned maintenance.

Painting the hull is not a cheap option and the decision to carry out this work depends partly on how long you intend to keep the boat and whether or not you would recoup the cost when you come to sell. See Chapter 15 for more information on painting the hull.

SAFETY PRECAUTIONS WHEN PREPARING TO PAINT

During the preparation stages a lot of dust is created. All dust is dangerous, especially that from old paints, antifouling and gel coats. Always wear the highest-quality face mask that you can buy. If your model uses replaceable filters, buy a stock and swap old for new according to the advice on the label. Use disposable rubber gloves. Your local DIY store probably sells them in packs of ten for about half the price of a box of a hundred from your paint supplier. Wear coveralls, disposable paper ones are best, a hat and goggles. If your coveralls do not have elasticated cuffs then tape the cuffs and wrist and ankles to your arms and legs with gaffer tape to prevent dust creeping in.

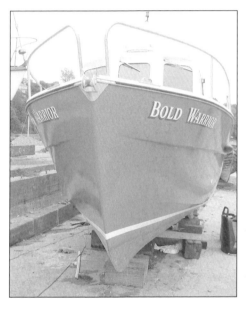

The hull of this motor launch has been hand-painted on the slip and the finish is as good as you would get from a professional yard.

Specialist work

If you need specialist maintenance done then it is always cheaper going directly to the people who do the work. If you ask a yard to carry out specialist machine work, or to check and repair the alternator or starter motor, or have the injectors tested and reset, then the likelihood is that they will take it to a specialist firm that actually does the work, add their mark up and send you the bill. Cut out the middleman and find your own specialist. Diesel specialists, for example, appear in *Yellow Pages* under car electrics or electric motors.

Sometimes the necessary expertise at the right price is found in the most unexpected places. This is a rural blacksmith's forge but he also works in stainless steel and here is seen making up a new stainless steel tiller.

◆ LEARNING THE SKILLS

Yacht maintenance is heavy on practical skills and light on theoretical knowledge. So if you know the theory but lack the practical skills, then take steps to acquire the necessary expertise. It will save you cash.

The following are relatively easy items to replace:

1 Fan belts
2 Impellers
3 Oil filters – not forgetting to change the oil at the same time as you change the oil filters
4 Fuel filters

Following the engine manufacturer's recommendations adds years to the life of your engine and greatly reduces the possibility of costly faults when far from home. To master this, together with winterising and then re-commissioning engines and generators, demands some low-level, easily acquired technical abilities and a working knowledge of fuel lines, filters, fan belts and electrical systems. If there is no one to show you how, then the cost and effort of learning these skills at an adult education class repays itself many times. If your local college does not hold classes on caring for marine diesels, they may well have a course on maintaining car and truck engines. The principles are exactly the same.

Similarly, you may find your local college offers courses on electrical installations, electronics, woodworking, painting or welding. Over a few winters you can build up a reasonable competence in a range of practical skills. Even if after all this training you still lack the skills required for a particular task, there is usually a lot of plain unskilled labouring work that you can manage. You can mix and match the work you can do with what you have to pay someone else to do. You might not be able to sew a new sacrificial strip on your roller furling headsail but you can buy a stitch ripper for pennies from the local dressmaking shop and take the old strip off. This cuts hours of labour charges from the sailmaker's bill.

Some yacht clubs have within their membership a wide range of practical skills which can be accessed on a co-operative basis. Tasks such as replacing an engine, the stern gland, or propshaft, an electrical rewire, stainless steel welding or tube bending that are beyond your knowledge and talents become possible with the freely given help of others who perhaps once earned their living doing this work. With their generous expert advice and help it is possible to carry out major repairs and modifications to a professional standard for the cost of the materials and a few beers, with the bonus that you have learned how to do it the next time.

Also within clubs where these skills are found is an encyclopaedic knowledge of local suppliers, specialists in every kind of field and the location of small machine shops hidden away where your small, one-off job is welcomed. If you are serious about saving money on maintenance then find one of these clubs and ask if they will have you as a member.

ANNUAL COSTS

No two boats, even if they are sister ships, have the same annual costs. Where you chose to berth and how much of the annual refit you do yourself will have an enormous effect on how much you pay out. Yachts should use less fuel than power boats and if you enjoy anchoring, then the overnight marina charges on your annual cruise will be much lower.

I spend more on overnight fees than on berthing charges. There are two reasons for this: first I have a yacht club mooring, and secondly I spend about four months cruising every season. What I spend on overnight fees represents about one night out of two in a marina.

The figures in the table below are a guide to where you can save cash and it is pretty obvious that there are three principal areas where this is possible:

1   **Berthing** Hunt around for the cheapest berth that suits you. The savings that can be made in this area are huge. Watch out for add-ons. Lifting out and winter storage can add a third to your berthing bill.

2   **DIY** The more work on your boat that you can do yourself (or by 'volunteers who work for an evening's beer) the more money you will save. The real cost of paying a yard is in labour charges, not materials.

3   **Anchoring** Anchoring not only saves money on your annual cruise and, when the weather suits, it is more peaceful.

A GUIDE TO ANNUAL COSTS – BASED ON A 32FT (9.75M) YACHT			
	DIY	Marina or boatyard	Remarks
Administration Club membership Harbour dues Insurance	£50.00 £25.00 £219.00	£50.00 £25.00 £219.00	
Berthing Annual berth	£300.00	£4536.68	Based on £402.00 per m + VAT at my local marina. The average charge in the UK is around £280 per metre.
Winter storage Lift out, wash and block off	£50.00	£289.73	Based on £25.84 per m & VAT
Pressure wash	Free	£25.00	
Lift in/wash	£50.00	£172.78	Based on £15.41 per m & VAT
Storage ashore Nov–Mar (154 days)	Free	£227.57	Based on £28.27 per m & VAT
Cradle hire	Free	£48.30	
Decommission engine	Free	£174.80	

	DIY	Marina or Boatyard	Remarks
Service engine (new belts/filters, oil etc)	£85.41	£174.80	
Check standing/running rigging	Free	£87.40	
Unstep mast and store on deck	Free	£131.75	Based on £11.75 per m & VAT
Travel Return travel from home to boat	£20.00	£20.00	Notional amount as I live 20 mins walk or 5 mins drive from my boat.
Routine annual refit Prepare under underwater area, apply antifoul (1 coat)	£50.00	£458.85	
Prepare brightwork, apply 2 coats yacht varnish	£10.00	£733.70	Yard cost assumes wood in good condition
Drive belt for water pump	£7.22	£13.39	Using compatible belts
Drive belt for alternator	£7.22	£13.39	and filters saves over
Fuel filter	£5.45	£10.70	£39.00 or almost 50%
Primary fuel filter	£6.50	£8.00	over the cost of branded
Impeller	£15.30	£29.43	items.
Oil filter	£4.50	£10.50	
Rolling programme – major refit	£150.00	£150.00	This is an average amount; some years more, others less.
Annual cruise Charts/pilot books Overnight berthing	£50.00 £665.00	£50.00 £665.00	I cruise for four months a year and spend only about one or two nights in a marina.
TOTAL COSTS	**£1,895.60**	**£8454.78**	These costs are based on my own DIY expenditure compared with estimated equivalent local marina costs, including labour.

15 | Painting the hull

One way that even an inexperienced boat owner on a budget can save substantial sums during the refit is to repaint the hull themselves – which is why I have included this subject as a separate chapter. Any keen owner who has some basic painting skills, plenty of stamina, and attention to detail, can tackle this job, provided that he or she use the correct materials and follow the instructions given. The secret of success is in meticulous preparation; you can use the very best paint system but if your preliminary work is not done thoroughly enough, and you apply the paint in the wrong atmospheric conditions, then you are actually wasting money not saving it.

◆ GENERAL ADVICE

Painting the hull on wood, steel and concrete boats is non-optional and on GRP boats it guards against the risk of osmosis. A good paint job protects the value of your boat for years. A poor paint job not only shows but it also has a short useful life before it must be completely stripped off and done again properly. Otherwise, water gets in and damages the hull.

Preparations
Careful preparation is essential for achieving a good paint finish but there is more to this than sanding the hull prior to painting. Preparations begin by carefully thinking through:

- How to prepare the hull for painting
- The paint system to be used
- How the paint is to be applied
- The conditions in which the paint is applied. This may determine when the work is done. If you wish to paint the hull in winter or early spring you may need to spend cash on tenting and heating the hull. Delaying the work until summer may save money
- Sourcing the materials and equipment that you will need at each stage of the work

Sourcing materials

Coatings on commercial vessels must really do the job well. If not, then the ship owners will seek redress. Individual yacht owners do not have this clout but can benefit from the fact that commercial marine products receive more testing and are likely to give better value and performance than their yachting equivalents. High performance coatings are not cheap but they will give a much longer working life than low-cost alternatives and prove less expensive in the end.

Check special offers on any paints carefully. They may be financially attractive but it is possible that the paint does not have extended overcoating times which means you will spend hours sanding the hull down between coatings or that it will not cure in the temperatures in which you apply it and you are forced to hire expensive heaters.

Costs

The price of the paints and other materials is around 10–15 per cent of the cost of a yard paint job. With care you save 80–90 per cent of the professional's price by doing the work yourself and still obtain a more than acceptable finish even if the work is done out of doors. As previously stated, a good finish depends mostly on how well you prepare the hull for painting. This is not a highly skilled task. It just requires endless patience, a cheerful acceptance of horrible working conditions and mind-numbing attention to small detail.

The paint system

Primer, undercoat and topcoat make up a single paint system and each should be compatible with the others; so do not mix and match coatings unless you are sure this is the case. A good paint system, properly applied, should result in a coating which has a life expectancy of 10 to 15 years with minimal annual maintenance. To be sure of buying the right system, speak to the technical (not the sales) department of your chosen paint manufacturer.

Quantities required

When estimating the quantities required, remember to make allowance for wastage and make sure that the solvents you need are specific to the materials you are using. These will be more expensive than 'white spirit' and other generic solvents.

You should always buy more paint than you think you need. There are formulae that can be used for calculating the coverage of any paint but turning theoretical answers into accurate estimates of the amount of paint required is complicated. The theory takes no account of the variable losses that will occur. Accurately judging the quantities required comes from hard-won experience. As a rough guide, losses come from:

1 Over-applying paint to achieve the specified minimum thickness. This varies with the method of application. When using brushes and rollers on simple structures it is probably around 5 per cent but can rise to as much as 15 per cent on complex structures. Excessive over-coating of modern high technology paints can lead to:
   - Solvent entrapment and subsequent loss of adhesion
   - Splitting of primer coats.
2 Spray painting can bring losses of 20 per cent on simple structures.
3 Paint dripping from brushes and rollers can largely be ignored but the equivalent spray painting losses can be considerable. As a rough guide, spraying losses:
   - In a well ventilated, confined space are around 5 per cent
   - Outdoors in still air are around 5–10 per cent
   - Outdoors in windy conditions are likely to be over 20 per cent
4 All paints have a 'pot life' and if a pot of paint is not used before this is reached then what remains is thrown away. The likely losses from this are:
   - Single-component paints, less than 5 per cent
   - Two-component paints, 5–10 per cent

It is best to buy your paints in five-litre (one-gallon) cans. Epoxy paints come as a large tin of base paint and a much smaller tin of hardener which together make up the five litres. The manufacturer's intention is that the entire tin of hardener is poured into the base paint and stirred in. A five-litre can is probably enough to coat the hull two or three times so mixing it all up according to the manufacturer's intentions will inevitably mean throwing away a lot of expensive paint. However, if you mix smaller quantities, it is important to observe the correct ratio of base to hardener. Buy a cheap plastic bucket and two plastic kitchen measuring jugs, one large for the base paint and a smaller one for the hardener. Measure base and hardener into the measuring jugs and pour both into the bucket. Mix thoroughly at each stage of this operation. A poor paint job can often be traced back to poor mixing.

Applying paint

It is quicker and easier to roll rather than brush paint onto the hull. Buy the largest packs of small four-inch rollers that you can find. Use them once and throw away. Begin by rolling vertically, then a cross patch of diagonal strokes and finally horizontally. The last few strokes should become ever lighter until you are barely touching the surface so that the paint flows into itself leaving a nice smooth finish. Paint the hull in sections about three or four feet wide and make sure that each new section is blended into its predecessor while the paint is still wet and rolls nicely. This also means you must paint the entire hull in one session. Do not paint part of the hull, allow the paint to cure, and then finish painting the hull on another occasion. The join will be visible for all to see.

Windless days are best for painting to avoid dust and grit blowing onto fresh paint. If you wish to protect the hull from this happening or you are using a spray gun, then erect a tent over your yacht. The owners of neighbouring boats may object to having your overspray freckle their hulls.

Overcoating times

The overcoating time is the interval between coats when you can apply another coat without the need to abrade or solvent wash the hull again to achieve suitable adhesion of subsequent coats. It is best to buy paints where the system compatibility includes extended overcoating times.

The minimum overcoating time appears on the manufacturer's data sheet. This is time that must be allowed for the drying and curing of a coating before applying the next coat of paint. Overcoating times vary with:

- The thickness of the paint coating
- The environmental conditions – especially in respect of temperature, humidity and ventilation.

Conditions during paint application

Do not apply paints when:

- Air temperature is below the drying or curing temperature of the paint
- In fog, mist or when precipitation is forecast
- When the hull is wet with condensation of if condensation is likely to occur during the drying period. Paints can tolerate high humidity but not if it leads to condensation forming

Extreme conditions are temperatures below 5°C (41°F) or above 40°C (104°F). Below 5°C the curing of two-pot epoxy paints slows down and can stop altogether and above 40°C the curing process is extremely rapid and care must be taken to avoid pinholes, voids, bubbles and poor coverage due to the rapid evaporation of the solvent.

Moisture readings

It is important to take moisture readings before working on wood, GRP and ferro-concrete hulls. These must be taken using a reliable Protimeter and not a cheap moisture meter from your local DIY store. The moisture readings for specific primers are available from the paint manufacturer's technical service division. As a rule of thumb, if the readings are above 4–5 per cent then if working outdoors, wait for better weather or move the vessel indoors (or tent it) and introduce a dehumidification system. Bringing in a heater is not sufficient. It only warms up the moisture in the hull.

Using heaters

If, for any reason, you wish to use a heater then be sure to use an indirect heating system. A direct heating system produces in the region of two kilograms of water for every kilogram of fuel burnt.

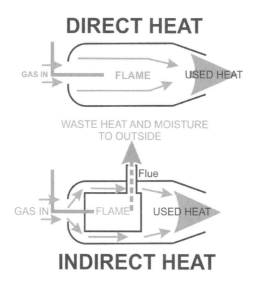

Tenting the hull

Tenting a hull needs a scaffolding framework and tarpaulins to cover it. If you cannot scrounge the scaffolding then you will need to hire it or build the framework from scrap 4x2 timber.

The cheapest possible tarpaulins will do but they must somehow be tied or fixed down to the framework at regular intervals, and the shorter the interval the better. The aim is to break down acres of tarpaulin into small squares so as to reduce the damage done to the tarpaulin by the wind. If this is not properly tied down, then pretty soon it will look like a sail shredded in a gale.

◆ WOODEN HULLS

Preparation

Strip back to the wood substrate (bare wood) by mechanical means, preferably hard scraping and sanding. Alternatives are:

- Controlled slurry blasting, which is expensive, may raise the grain and the moisture content must be checked afterwards.
- Using paint strippers which can only remove two or three coats per application. Depending on the number of coatings what first appeared to be a £50 job may prove to be three or four times as expensive. Also, it is not a good idea to put new paint on top of wood contaminated with paint stripper so its *complete* removal is essential.

Once the bare wood is reached, a final sanding is necessary to achieve as good a surface as possible. Prominent grain not only reduces coating thickness but can poke through the paint and provide a wick for moisture penetration into the hull.

Moisture readings should not exceed 18 per cent before painting and all knots in the wood sealed. All nail holes and crevices should be filled using a solvent-free pure epoxy filler.

If you are certain that the existing coating is a properly applied epoxy paint and you know what sort of epoxy it is, then it may be possible to overcoat it. If it is an oleo-resinous paint (yacht enamel) then overcoating is not advisable as the final result will have a much shorter useful life. On older craft you may encounter a chlorinated rubber coating which is treated in the same manner as oleo-resinous coatings.

Paint system

You can use epoxy or similar high performance paints, oleo-resinous (yacht enamel) paints or acrylics. On a scale of one to ten, oleo-resinous and acrylic paints rate around a seven and epoxies a ten.

◆ GRP HULLS

Preparation

Once old coatings, including antifouling, have been removed *carefully*, abrade the gel coat. A low-pressure slurry blast or a dry low-pressure blast is better than sanding, and depending on the size of vessel, hiring the equipment to do this task can avoid weeks of sanding.

Once this work is done, you can check the hull for any minor scrapes and bangs and stress-point crazing around bulkheads and fittings. Such damage should be made good before painting. Filling of cracks etc should be with a solvent-free, pure epoxy filler, not car filler which is bulked out with china clay and talc and is unsuitable for marine use.

The moisture content of the hull should not exceed 4–5 per cent.

Paint system

Use an epoxy or similar high performance system. If possible, ensure that the topside finish be readily overcoated in case of subsequent bumps and scrapes damaging the finish. Some polyurethane and siloxane paints are not user-friendly in this respect.

◆ STEEL HULLS

Preparation

Grit blasting is the best way to remove old coatings from a steel hull. You can either dry or wet blast or use an ultra-high-pressure water blast although this is not really an option for the amateur. It is expensive and as it operates at a pressure of around 3000 bar, it can push in the plating, revealing every frame and stiffener.

Wet blasting can result in 'flash' rust. However, there are primers which are specifically designed to be applied directly to 'flash' rusted surfaces and these should be used if you opt for wet blasting.

Whatever method is used make sure that awkward areas such as those around stanchions and fittings are thoroughly blasted as entrapped corrosion can weaken the final finish.

To give the paint system a good physical 'key' the blasting should result in a surface profile of about 50 microns. It is important that the primer thickness makes allowance for this as the protection it gives needs to be above the 'peaks' of the profile.

SURFACE PROFILE AMPLITUDE
The difference between the peaks and troughs created by blast-cleaning is called the amplitude and expressed in microns. The amplitude must be enough to ensure good adhesion but if it is too great it means higher paint consumption and the risk of some peaks poking through the paint, resulting in 'peak rashing' or spot rusting.

Paint applied to a properly blast-cleaned surface can be expected to last five times longer that a surface which has been manually wire brushed. There are standards for levels of cleanliness. It is usual for steel to be blast-cleaned to Swedish Standard SIS 05 59 00 – Sa 2.5 or its equivalent British Standard (BS 7079 Part 1A) or that of the Steel Structures Painting Council of America.

Prior to blasting, the hull should be degreased using a biodegradable water soluble degreaser before painting to remove all soluble salts, grease, drilling and cutting compounds. This wash must be followed by thoroughly wiping with clean rags.

On older and home-built boats, it is possible that when preparing the hull for blasting some blistering of the existing paint is observed. It looks rather like (but obviously is not) osmosis. The most likely cause is that after the original steel was shot blasted at the mill it was given a PVB coating. Subsequently, moisture has penetrated between the coating and the steel and created PVB blisters. Their presence justifies the total removal of the existing coatings rather than quicker and cheaper spot blasting which will not cure the basic problem.

If the blasting reveals any corrosion pitting in the plates then these should be filled in with a solvent-free, pure epoxy filler, not car filler which is bulked out with china clay and unsuitable for marine use.

Paint system

Although your boat may be wintered ashore, make sure that the paint system is recommended as suitable for full time immersion and is resistant to cathodic disbondment. This is important on steel-hulled vessels.

◆ ALUMINIUM HULLS

Preparation

Depending on the grade of aluminium, the topsides can be left untreated, especially on high speed craft. However, underwater areas will need treating and antifouling to prevent barnacles and seaweed growth.

Remove any existing coatings using chemical paint strippers and clean the areas to be painted with high pressure (jet) hot water detergent wash and then rinse or, alternatively, scrub with an emulsifier degreaser. When using a jet wash, the best results are achieved by keeping the nozzle close to the hull; 'backing off' may speed up the work but dissipates the energy from the jet wash and the result is a poorer finish.

It is also good practice to lightly abrade the aluminium before applying the paint. Scotchbrite-type pads are good on light sheet but 80 to 120 grit aluminium oxide flexible pads on orbital sanders are better on heavier material. Using any other kind of sanding pads can result in their residue leading to electrolysis.

The aluminium powder that sanding creates must be removed before painting.

If the blasting reveals any corrosion pitting in the plates, as with steel, then these should be filled in with a solvent-free, pure epoxy filler. Don't use car filler which is bulked out with china clay and talc and is unsuitable for marine use.

A thin coat of a proprietary acid etch primer should be applied prior to painting. This provides a key for subsequent coats. The acid etch primer should change from pale yellow to a greenish brown. If this does not happen then the hull must be scraped clean, treated with a proprietary aluminium pre-treatment solution and the acid etch primer re-applied.

Paint system

The primer in particular, but preferably the entire paint system, should be di-electrically inert. In practice this means that there should be no metallic content in any of the coatings as this could encourage electrolysis.

◆ FERRO-CEMENT HULLS

Preparation

The hull should be clean, dry and free from oil, grease, lubricants and curing components which will affect paint adhesion. The moisture content of the cement should be less than 6 per cent. Paint on hulls with higher readings result in blistering and flaking as the trapped moisture slowly escapes.

If it is a new hull then you must remove all surface laitence (milky deposit) using a sweep blast or low pressure wash. Surface laitence and loose surface powder are always found on new cement.

If there are existing coatings, remove them using a chemical paint stripper and then low-pressure wash. Be careful with the wash. If the moisture readings are above 6 per cent you will have to introduce dehumidification or wait until they have dropped to an acceptable level before applying the primer.

Paint system

Use an epoxy or similar high performance system. If possible, ensure that the topside finish is readily overcoated in case of subsequent bumps and scrapes damaging the finish. Some polyurethane and siloxane paints are not user-friendly in this respect.

Paint manufacturers and suppliers

The simplest way of preparing a list of paint suppliers in your area is to open your favourite search engine, enter 'marine paint manufacturers and suppliers' taking care to add Great Britain, the USA or any country of your choice. You can then shop around for the best price. It is unlikely that the manufacturer of a particular brand of paint will supply to you directly but they, or their web site, will tell you where you can find the nearest supplier.

In the USA the NPCA, a voluntary, non-profit trade association that has been going for over a century, is the pre-eminent organisation in the United States representing paint and coatings manufacturers, raw materials suppliers and distributors. It has an online Member Directory primarily designed for people in the paint, coatings, or chemical industry but is also a great way of finding your favourite paint manufacturer. It is found at www.paint.org/index.htm

A list of useful addresses for marine paint specialists can be found overleaf.

USEFUL ADDRESSES OF MARINE PAINT SPECIALISTS

INTERNATIONAL PAINTS
Stoneygate Lane
Felling
Gateshead
Tyne & Wear
NE10 0JY
44 (0) 191 469 6111
44 (0) 191 438 3711

INTERNATIONAL PAINT LLC
4730 Crittenden Drive
Louisville
Kentucky 40209
+1 502 375 5593
+1 502 375 5595
www.internationalpaint.com

ICI
ICI is now part of Akzo Nobel which also controls International Paints. Their Trade Technical Advice Centre at ICI's headquarters in Slough has a team of technical experts knowledgeable and trained in all aspects of ICI Trade Paints. The centre handles thousands of incoming telephone calls, letters, faxes and internet enquiries from trade customers every week. Literature, colour and product advice and system recommendations are available from the centre. The ICI Specifier hotline number in the UK is 44 (0) 175 369 1690

JOTUN PAINTS (EUROPE) LTD
Stather Road
Flixborough, Scunthorpe
North Lincolnshire
DN15 8RR
England
Tel: 44 (0) 172 440 0000
Fax: 44 (0) 172 440 0100

HEMPEL PAINTS LTD
Llantarnam Industrial Park
Cwmbran
Gwent
NP4 3XF
Tel: 44 (0) 163 387 4024
Fax: 44 (0) 163 348 9089

LEIGH PAINTS
Tower Works
Kestor Street
Bolton
BL2 2AL
Tel: 44 (0) 120 452 1771
Fax: 44 (0) 120 438 2115

Appendix: Buying a boat – the formalities

When you buy a boat, whether new or second-hand, it is very much a case of 'Buyer Beware!' This appendix looks at the points you should consider before you close the deal. The law varies so much that it is not possible to cover every country here so this is mostly viewed from the UK perspective. However, every country has similar laws and the principles it describes hold good everywhere. Also covered are aide-memoires on the points that should be included in the contracts for new and second-hand boats respectively and their purpose is to remind you to tick off these points before shaking hands and declaring the purchase a done deal.

In the UK, yachts are chattels and not, like houses, property. This limits your rights. Second-hand boats bought directly from a private individual come with no warranty and scope for redress is very limited. The Misrepresentation Act 1967 makes it an offence for the seller to make false claims about the goods they are selling. Boats bought through yards, brokers and distributors come under the Sale of Goods Act 1979, as amended by the Sale and Supply of Goods Act 1994. The important points are:

- *Section 12* The seller has the right to sell
- *Section 13* The goods are accurately described
- *Section 14* The goods are fit for purpose

This is all very interesting but in the real world you will almost certainly have to go to court for it to have any force if you are sold a pup. Going to court is costly and the only real beneficiaries are the lawyers. That said, reminding the seller of the existence of the law may be a useful negotiating point if you are having difficulty escaping from a deal that has gone bad.

◆ BUYING A NEW BOAT

A new yacht may be custom-built at a yard of your choice or bought through a distributor. Yards and distributors gladly provide contracts for you to sign but being human it is only to be expected that wherever possible these contracts favour the yard or distributor. This is mostly achieved by laying down your commitments, especially those regarding payments, in rigorous detail and leaving theirs surrounded by sufficient uncertainty to provide them room to manoeuvre over any point they choose. Fortunately the BMF offer a standard form contract that aims to strike a balance between vendor and buyer which many boatyards use. Read every contract carefully, looking to see if it covers the points listed on page 132. If not, negotiate until you are happy with the contract.

◆ BUYING A SECOND-HAND BOAT

Life is more complicated when you buy a second-hand boat. There is far more work involved and more pitfalls to avoid. If you are buying through a broker then you can ask him to provide written confirmation that the boat is not stolen, and that it is the vendor's to sell and is free of debt. Often all you will receive is a statement beginning, *as far as we can ascertain . . .* which is understandable but unhelpful. You could ask the broker to list the checks, and their results, which led him to make this statement and if you are still unhappy then you must check matters out yourself. It is not difficult and you would have to do these checks if you were buying directly from an individual.

◆ REGISTRATION

Every country has its own rules on small craft registration and checking if a boat is registered is one way of establishing that the boat is the vendor's to sell.

Unless going abroad, yachts based in the UK need not be registered and until 1983, when the Small Ships Register (SSR) was introduced, all registered yachts were on the Part 1 register. This proves ownership for the last five years. The SSR does not prove ownership.

In the USA, a vessel registered with the US Coast Guard is called a documented vessel. To be documented, a yacht must be five net tons or more and owned by a US national. Net tonnage is a measure of volume, not weight, and as a rough guide, a yacht of 25ft LOA qualifies.

Full details of the documentation regulations can be found at http://bookstore.gpo.gov/ and application forms for documentation can be downloaded from http://www.uscg.mil/hq/g-m/vdoc/genpub.htm.

Undocumented recreational vessels in the USA must be registered in the state of principal use. This is done through the State Boating Law Administrator who gives the boat a unique number that is displayed on the hull and issues a certificate which must be carried aboard the boat. Some states may require documented yachts to be registered with them and although they do not have to display a state number they may be required to display a notice saying that they have met the state requirements.

◆ DEBTS AND CHARGES

A vessel's debts are transferred to the new owner when it is sold. Debts include outstanding payments for work done, berthing fees or outstanding balances on loans for which the boat has been used as collateral. Marine mortgages can appear on a ship's papers if it is a documented vessel (USA) or the Part 1 register (UK) but not the SSR.

Debts also include fines. Nowadays authorities are taking a harder line on environmental damage caused by garbage, oil and fuel spills and can levy substantial fines. If these are not paid before a boat changes hands then they can seize the boat from the new owner and hold it until outstanding fines are paid.

It is essential that, before completing the sale, you obtain a written declaration from the vendor that the boat is free of all debts and charges.

◆ HULL IDENTIFICATION NUMBERS

Hull Identification Numbers (HINs) first appeared in the USA in 1972 and in the UK in the 1980s. In 1996 boatbuilders in about 70 countries adopted the International Organisation for Standardisation (ISO) HIN scheme which gives each boat an unique 12 digit number made up of:

- The boat's hull number
- The builder's number
- The date the boat was certified to meet manufacturing regulations
- Its model year

European builders must also add a two-digit country code.

Some authorities believe that HINs should be increased to 17 digits, removing anomalies between countries and bringing them in line with the international system for Vehicle Identification Numbers (VINs).

HINs are moulded into a vessel's transom. In the UK, from 2001

RFID labelling is used. This is a small silicon chip embedded in the hull which carries details of the boat and its ownership which can be read electronically. RFID labelling is less susceptible to tampering.

If a boat is stolen there is a good chance that the HIN will have been altered. For moulded HINs there is no agreed typeface so that some letters and numerals can be easily, and sometimes deliberately, confused. Moulded HIN numbers on the transom can be altered, painted over or obscured by fixing equipment over them. HINs can be checked on http://www.boatfax.com.

In the UK, HINs can also be checked through the Boatmark Scheme which was introduced in 1995 by the British Marine Federation and HPI, a company which runs the motor trade's VIN anti-fraud database. Boat owners registering with the scheme receive a certificate which can then be checked by prospective buyers. The advantage of the Boatmark Scheme is that it is retrospective and older boats which would not normally have a HIN can be registered. It was hoped that marine mortgages and loans for boats would be registered with the Boatmark Scheme, but take up has been poor, possibly because there are charges for using it.

◆ STOLEN BOATS

Some owners visit their boat so infrequently it could be stolen, sailed halfway round the world and sold several times before they notice it is missing. In the UK around 10 to 20 boats are stolen each day. This is trivial compared to motor vehicle theft, but if you buy a stolen boat and the police, insurers or owners track it down, you can lose it without receiving a penny in compensation even if you bought it in good faith.

Reduce the risk of this happening by checking the vessel's paperwork. The registration documents should match the hull identification number as should the numbers in the technical documents for items such as the engine. Bear in mind that the documentation may not keep pace with engines being replaced but if the numbers do not match then always ask why.

These checks are more difficult with unregistered boats and older boats which may not have HINs or the paperwork that goes with meeting the RCD. There is no legal requirement to insure your boat but adequate third party cover is a condition for renting most marina berths. Ask to see the current insurance certificate and investigate further if it is not forthcoming or if the vendor's name and address or the boat's name do not match those on the paperwork.

In the UK, many boats are registered with the Coastguard CG66 scheme which holds the boat's details along with the owner's name and address and, often, a photograph of the boat. This is done to help the Coastguard should the vessel ever require assistance. It is in an owner's (self) interest to make sure the details are accurate and up-to-date and they can check and amend their entry on line. Ask the vendor if his boat is registered with the scheme, and if it is, go on line with him to view his details.

Consult lists of stolen boats. The principal website for this in the UK is www.stolenboats.org.uk. This was set up in 2005 and all UK police forces and marine insurers enter details of boats that they know are stolen. This information can be accessed free of charge. Various insurance companies and other organisations also have lists of stolen boats on their websites.

◆ CONTRACTS FOR SECOND-HAND BOATS

When you buy a second-hand boat there should be a buyer's contract which each party signs. This will be your purchase receipt and prove that you are the new owner. Some websites allow you to download sample contracts but fine tune them to meet your particular circumstances. Points to look for are listed on page 135. The devil is in the detail. Misread the small print of a contract and you may find yourself liable for someone else's unpaid debts or subsequently have your right to ownership called into question.

◆ VAT

Within the EU there must be evidence that Value Added Tax (VAT) has been paid or an acceptable reason why the vessel is exempt from paying VAT. Other countries will have their own system of taxes applicable to yachts. From your point of view it is important that you receive acceptable proof that all taxes have been paid or you may find the taxman nailing a writ to the mast.

As with all government regulations, the rules on the VAT status of yachts are complicated. If you are in any doubt about whether or not VAT has been paid or is due to be paid then check with HM Revenue and Customs. Do this before committing yourself to buying the boat in question. HM Revenue and Customs will tell you what they will consider acceptable evidence that VAT has been paid and you can request the vendor to provide it. In the UK, HM Revenue and Customs can be found at www.hmrc.gov.uk. Broadly, the rules are as follows:

Acceptable evidence that VAT has been paid is:

1 Original purchase receipt
2 Documentary evidence that VAT was paid at the time the boat was imported into the EEA
3 Invoices for the materials and equipment used to construct DIY boats

Exemptions

If a boat was used as a private vessel before 1 January 1985 *and* located in the EU before 31 December 1992, VAT is 'deemed' to have been paid under age-related relief. Acceptable evidence that a vessel is exempt from paying VAT is in two parts:

1 For age of vessel
   - Marine Survey
   - Part 1 Registration
   - Insurance Certificates
   - Builder's Certificate

2 For location before 31 December 1992
   - Receipts for moorings, marina berths or harbour dues
   - Dry dock or yard storage receipts

Imported vessels

Yachts, whether new or second-hand, bought outside the EU must pay VAT regardless of age or previous tax history. They may also be liable for import duty. Charges are payable at the first port of call in the EU

Imported within EU

If you buy a new boat in one EU country to keep in another EU country, VAT becomes payable in the country where you intend to keep it

Exported vessels

Under the Sailaway Boat Scheme you can buy a yacht tax free in the EU if you sail under its own power to a country outside the EU

TAXES IN THE USA

In the USA, a sales tax, based on a percentage of the purchase price, is added onto the price of goods or services bought in the USA. Almost every state has a sales tax. The exceptions are Alaska, Delaware, Montana, New Hampshire and Oregon but they have an equivalent 'use' or property tax.

If you buy a boat in a no-tax state and then use it in a taxing state, that state will want you to pay 'use' tax. Some states require marinas to report your presence. Marine patrol and harbourmasters may ask to see tax stickers. Documenting your boat federally doesn't make it immune from taxes. Hawaii has a form of sales tax called a General Excise Tax (GET) which is charged on businesses rather than consumers, although in the end the consumer pays. In some places sales taxes are assessed at county or municipal level.

CHECKLIST FOR BUYING A SECOND-HAND BOAT IN THE USA

When you buy a second-hand boat in the USA, the sequence of actions goes something like:

1 Go to the US Coastguard Documentation Centre (www.uscg.mil and follow the links) and download the forms and the instructions for completing them for:
  a) Exchange of documentation
  b) Release of lien (this assumes that there is outstanding loan or charge on the boat you intend to buy)
  c) Bill of Sale

2 Take the time to make yourself familiar with these forms.

3 Insist that the seller either:
  a) Gives the check for the deposit and paper work to a marine escrow company. This is the marine equivalent to a real estate escrow company. They charge a fee but they tell you the amount up front and you and the seller can agree to who pays what. The marine escrow handle all the financial movements and as part of its service, conducts a search of liens against the vessel, outstanding loans, collecting and paying to the state any applicable sales taxes etc. You and the seller agree a closing date, fill out and sign the paperwork (see below) but the marine escrow company does the work.

or
  b) introduces you to the bank which holds the loan and you make sure that you have the name and contact details of whoever is dealing with this matter and the seller has told them that you are the purchaser.

4 Ask the bank to tell you, in writing, how much the loan will be on the date you plan to exchange contracts and close the deal. At the same time ask them for instructions on how to wire the money to them and pass these onto your bank.

5 Fill in the USCG's
   a) Application for Exchange of Documentation
   b) Bill of Sale

6 On the date you have chosen for closing the deal:
   a) Give the seller a check for the agreed amount, less any deposit and the outstanding loan.
   b) Instruct your bank to wire the amount of the outstanding loan to the seller's bank. There will be a charge for this but the alternative is waiting for the seller to receive your check, pay in into his bank and instruct them to pay off the loan.
   c) Both you and the seller complete and sign two original notarised Bills of Sale using the USCG form. The USCG insist on their form being used. You can photocopy the completed forms but the signatures and notary's seal on each form must be original.
   d) The seller gives you the boat's documentation.

7 You are now a proud boat owner who now has to:
   a) Make copies of the original Bills of Sale and Application for Exchange of Documentation
   b) Send the originals to the USCG
   c) Call your contact at the seller's bank to confirm that they have sent the Coast Guard a release of lien form. Do this every day until they confirm this has been done.

8 Wait for the Coast guard to send you the new documentation.

CHECKING A CONTRACT FOR A NEW BOAT

The price

Is the price fixed? Are there extras in the contract over and above the agreed price? Have items like Delivery and Commissioning appeared? One-word items such as 'commissioning' must have their individual elements itemised and priced.

The delivery date

Is the delivery date fixed? Are there (cash) penalties for late delivery? Agree acceptable reasons for delays and list them in the contract. Otherwise, delays invoke the penalty clause.

Arbitration

Is there an agreed means of arbitration? It is a good idea to insist on this for it allows differences to be resolved without the expense of going to court.

Ownership

When does ownership of the vessel pass to you? Insist that costly items of equipment such as masts, engines and electronics, bought by the builder using your cash, but not yet installed on your boat, are clearly marked as owned by you. If ownership is unclear then should the builder go bust the receiver would regard your boat and its associated equipment as company assets and you as an unsecured creditor are at the bottom of the food chain.

Specification

If you are buying a one-off design then the specification must lay down every detail of the construction of the yacht, the materials to be used and the make and model of all the equipment up to and including the teaspoons in the cutlery drawer. Sometimes less reputable yards sell equipment and fittings rejected by other buyers to their next customer. If you have not specified otherwise, then you are stuck with it.

If you are buying a production yacht, will the specification be the same as that of the demonstration model which helped you decide to buy this boat? Some contracts allow manufacturers to change the specification without reference to you. There are often good reasons for changes but you should be made aware of these and agree to them, particularly if they involve expensive items such as:

- Construction and lay up of hull
- Engines and generators
- Mast and rigging
- Deck fittings
- Internal accommodation

If you cannot reach agreement over proposed changes to the specification, then you should be able to pull out of the deal with all monies paid returned in full.

Delivery

Where do you take delivery of the finished boat? This matters if the boat is being built abroad or at some distance from its intended berth.

Sea trials

Is there provision for sea trials? These are especially important for non-production yachts. Leisure craft sea trials normally last no more than half a day. This is not enough. Without a retention (see below) sea trials are your only opportunity to check out the boat and its systems. It would be prudent to negotiate longer and more meaningful sea trials before signing the contract.

Staged payments

A common sequence of payments for new build is

5/10%	Paid as a deposit
30/40%	Paid on completion of hull
30/40%	Paid on completion of fitting out
10/20%	Paid on completion of sea trials.

For a production yacht, there is a substantial deposit and the balance on delivery.

Retentions

Is there provision for holding onto some of the cash (a retention) for an agreed period after you have taken delivery so that you can satisfy yourself the yacht performs as promised? A retention of around 5–10 per cent for one sailing season is a prudent back-up to any guarantee the builder or distributor may offer.

Insurance

Is the builder's insurance adequate to cover your yacht while it is being built? This is particularly important if you have taken over ownership. If in doubt, arrange your own insurance.

Other parties

If you are buying through a distributor, your contract is with the distributor, not the boatyard or manufacturer. You have no legal options against the builder even if, in the event of defects appearing, the distributor encourages you to deal directly with the manufacturer. Agents and distributors go bust and, if this happens, raising problems over any cash that you have paid in advance could be especially difficult to resolve if the agent is based in another country.

Regulation compliant

In the UK, yachts must comply with various EU Directives, be CE compliant and come with their allocation of technical data books. If you intend to use the vessel for commercial purposes there are more regulations and Codes of Practice to meet. The need to comply with all appropriate rules, regulations and Codes of Practice must be spelt out in the contract.

Tax status

Who is responsible for ensuring that all taxes due are paid? Where is the evidence this has happened?

BUYING A SECOND-HAND BOAT

Contact details

Obtain full contact details for the vendor (seller). Check this is the vendor's actual address. If it is a business address it may be that, for tax purposes, the boat is owned by a company even though you believe that you are buying from an individual. This may leave you open to unpaid taxes or require the approval of the company shareholders before the vendor can sell what is legally a company asset. Be wary of anyone offering only a post office box number and a mobile telephone number as their contact details. If the vendor lives in one country and is selling a boat in another, ask why and be wary if there is no satisfactory explanation.

Legal position

If buying abroad, specify the country under whose laws the contract is made. Never assume that the contract law of one country is the same as any other. If you are buying abroad consider appointing your own, independent local agent/lawyer familiar with the local yachting scene and local laws to act on your behalf.

Right to sell

Has the vendor the right to sell the boat? If the boat is owned by a partnership or consortium there must be written evidence of agreement by all concerned that the individual you are dealing with has their authority to sell the boat and to receive payment for it.

Debt free

You need confirmation that the vessel is free of all debts and charges and later, if any are discovered relating to events before the date of sale, that they are the responsibility of the vendor.

Tax position

Have all taxes due, including import duty if the boat was originally imported, been paid in full? Has VAT been paid on the vessel or is the vessel exempt from VAT? Be very wary of proceeding if the vendor cannot provide the necessary documentation showing taxes have been paid.

Regulation compliant

Is there paperwork confirming that the vessel complies with the Recreational Craft Directive and all and any other applicable regulations?

The price

Obtain confirmation of the agreed selling price and that it has been paid in full.

As advertised

During the sales phase there are floods of glossy verbal statements and shiny promises. Subsequent disagreements over exactly what was claimed or promised are avoided by asking for all claims in writing.

Sea trials

Ensure there is agreement on what amounts to satisfactory sea trials before purchase is completed and any payments are made.

Remedial work

In your price negotiations, the vendor may promise to carry out some remedial work. You need evidence that any repairs the seller has agreed to carry out as a result of your negotiations have been made in a professional manner, to a satisfactory standard by a mutually agreed contractor. It is better that you do this work yourself and cover its cost by negotiating a reduction in the price.

◆ YACHT CONSTRUCTION STANDARDS

Most countries have regulations specifying minimum construction standards for leisure vessels. As yachting becomes more of a global market, there are moves towards an agreed international standard that harmonises ABYC standards (American Boat & Yacht Council) for products placed on the USA market with those of the ISO (International Organization for Standardization) and the European Recreational Craft Directives.

Standards in the USA

Yachts built in the USA must comply with the provisions of Federal Laws in Title 33 of the Code of Federal Regulations (commonly known as 33 CFR). You can get a copy from the US Coast Guard at the Marine Safety Office in Washington, DC. The USCG also issue Hull Identification Numbers (HIN).

The American Boat and Yacht Council (ABYC) (www.abycinc.org) publish voluntary construction and equipment standards. The ABYC is a not-for-profit organisation that has been developing, writing and updating the safety standards for boat building and repair in the United States for over 50 years and is actively involved with the International Organization for Standardization (ISO). As a rule, boats that meet all of the ABYC standards also comply with the Federal Standards.

European Recreational Craft Directives

Recreational Craft Directives 94/25/EC and 2003/44/EC apply to all leisure craft between 2.5 and 24 metres LOA, whether fully built or partly completed, and cover all aspects of construction including strength of construction, stability, electrical, fuel and gas systems. Complying with the stability requirements may require the boat be assessed against the ISO 12217 Standard on stability and buoyancy.

These rules apply to boats in the European Economic Area (EEA) which is all EU countries and their dependent territories plus Norway and Iceland. They came into force on 16 June 1996 with a two-year transition period before they became mandatory. During this time builders could either comply with the new regulations or with any other existing, applicable standards.

The directives apply to boats constructed in the EU or imported into the EU from elsewhere. The builder, the importer, the owner or whoever puts the boat into use in the EU can all be held responsible for confirming that the boat meets all the required standards and carries the appropriate CE marking.

The practical effect of the directives is that after 16 June 1998 all boats must comply with the directives and be CE marked. This includes second-hand vessels built outside the EU and sold in the EU after 16 June 1998.

If you are concerned that a boat you wish to buy should comply but does not have the right paperwork to comply with these directives, or if you are in any doubt about its CE status, then check – otherwise you may end up paying to have it surveyed and to bring it up to standard if it does not comply.

◆ SAILING WATERS

The RCD also place boats into one of four categories of sailing waters:

Category	Suitable for	Mean wave height
A	Ocean sailing	Over 4 metres
B	Offshore sailing	Between 2 and 4 metres
C	Inshore sailing	Between 0.5 and 2.0 metres
D	Sheltered water sailing	Up to 0.5 metres

Index